Floral Collection
for Hand Embroidery
An Embroiderers Garden

Maria Diaz

Tuva Publishing

www.tuvapublishing.com

Address Merkez Mah. Cavusbasi Cad. No:71
Cekmekoy - Istanbul 34782 / Turkey
Tel: +9 0216 642 62 62

Floral Collection for Hand Embroidery
An Embroiderers Garden

First Print 2014 / November
Second Print 2017 / August

All Global Copyrights Belong To
Tuva Tekstil ve Yayıncılık Ltd.

Content Embroidery

Editor in Chief Ayhan DEMİRPEHLİVAN
Project Editor Kader DEMİRPEHLİVAN
Designer Maria DİAZ
Technical Editors Leyla ARAS, Büşra ESER
Graphic Designers Ömer ALP, Abdullah BAYRAKÇI
Assistant Zilal ÖNEL
Photograph Tuva Publishing

ISBN 978-605-5647-63-6

Printing House
Bilnet Matbaacılık ve Yayıncılık. A.Ş.

Introduction

I am delighted to introduce to you this my first book of Embroidery designs from Tuva Publishing. This book contains lots and lots of beautiful embroidery patterns for hand embroidery.

Although each pattern does have a colour key and stitch suggestion indicated, I do hope the versatility of each design is evident. From novice using these simple outlines you could create lovely pieces just using backstitch or to the more experienced stitcher can ignite there creativity by filling the shapes with any number of different stitches.

With some pretty florals to a few more fun motif based designs. If a variety of sizes they can be used in any number of ways, to adorn table cloths, towels and cushions, to clothing. Why not test your imagination and put them together to produce an original sampler all of your own.

Maria Diaz

TOOLS

Embroidery is a wonderful hobby, even on the go because the materials needed are fairly minimal. All you really need is a needle, thread and fabric, although there are a few other basic tools that will help. I have put together a simple list to get you started.

Dress makers shears or large scissors, for cutting fabric.

Cross stitch or tapestry needles, have blunt tips these are much better when working on wider weave fabrics such a linen, hardanger or Aida.

Embroidery transfer pen or pencil, to draw or trace the designs onto fabric.

Embroidery or small sharp scissors, for snipping the thread as you stitch..

Needle threader, always useful when sewing.

Embroidery hoop, these come in a wide range of sizes and are easy to use.

Dressmakers pins, to keep pattern in place whilst tracing

Tape measure, to help position design

Needles, there are many types of needle but here are the two most commonly used:

Embroidery needles, best for fine work as they have very sharp points great essential when stitching on cotton or silk fabrics.

Tapestry frame, perfect for larger projects instead of using a hoop you can secure your work to the frame until it is finished.

TIP

You should bind the inner ring to help protect you fabric, another good tip is to always remove your embroidery when you are not working on it., this will help ensure you do not stretch your fabric into a permanent ring shape.

FABRICS

Freehand embroidery is so versatile it can be stitched onto virtually anything but I would suggest starting simply with a plain weave fabric.

Plain weave fabrics - cotton, linen or silk for example.

Evenweave fabric - hardanger, Aida, are just a couple, these purpose made fabric where the same number of threads are woven vertically and horizontally. These are great if you are combining freestyle embroidery with a more regimented stitch to create a border for example.

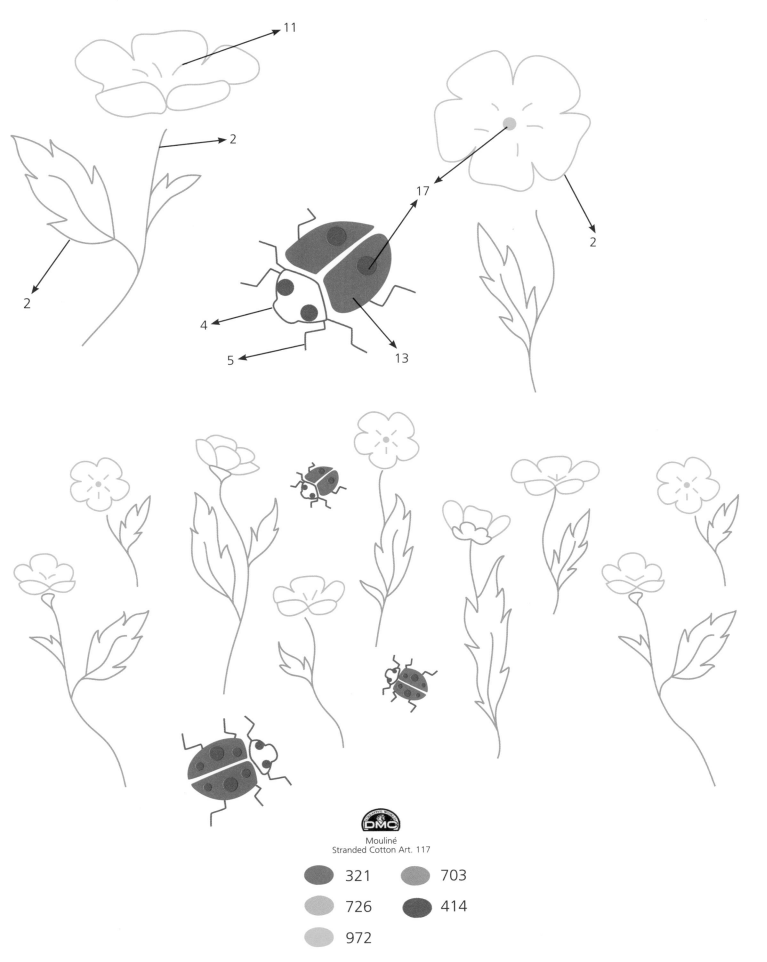

11

2

2

2

17

4

5

13

DMC

Mouliné
Stranded Cotton Art. 117

321   703

726   414

972

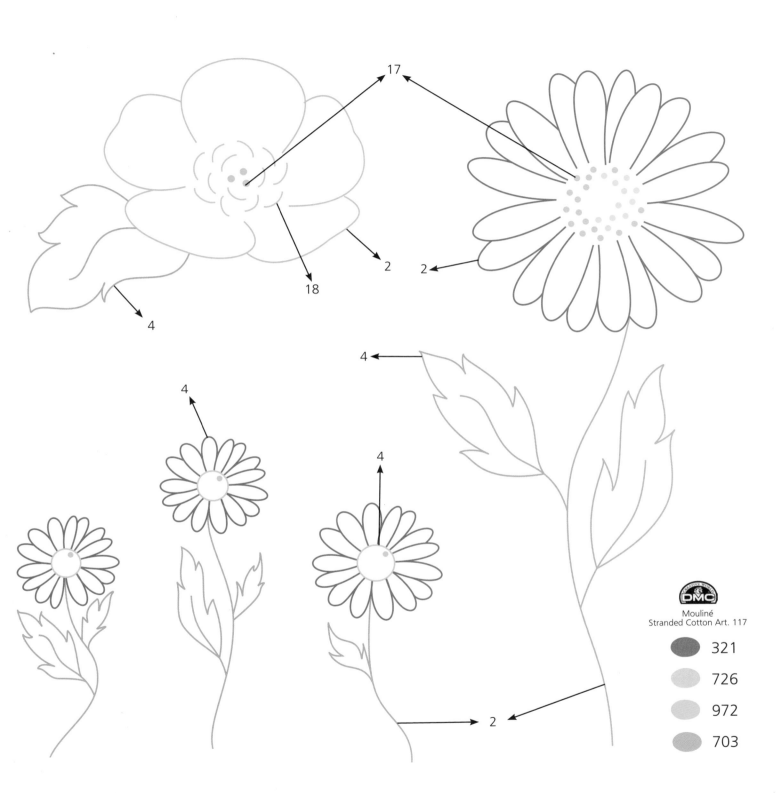

17

2

18

4

2

2

4

4

4

DMC
Mouliné
Stranded Cotton Art. 117

321
726
972
703

2

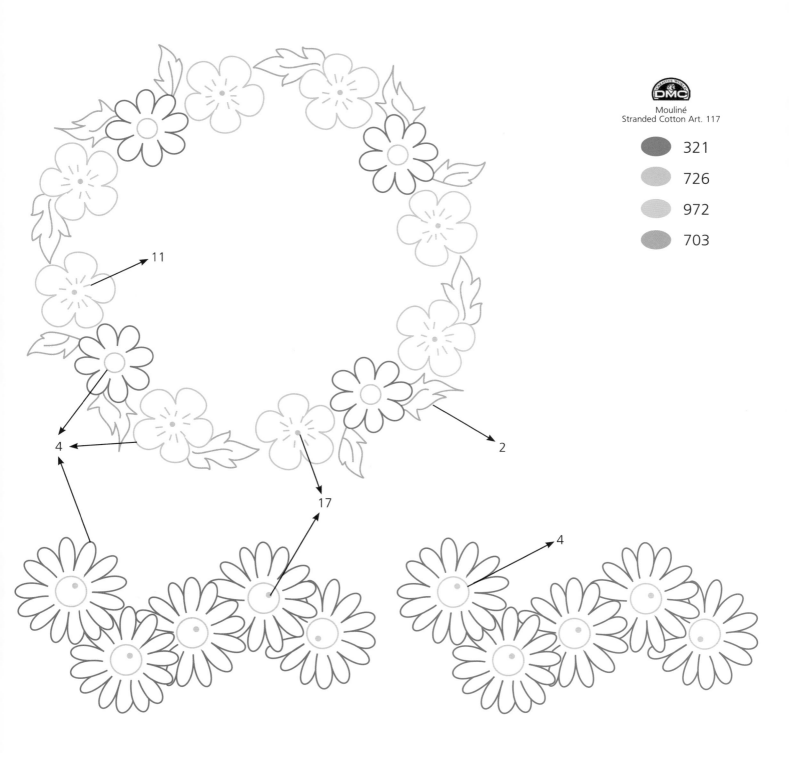

Mouliné
Stranded Cotton Art. 117

321
726
972
703

Mouliné
Stranded Cotton Art. 117

321
726
972
703
414

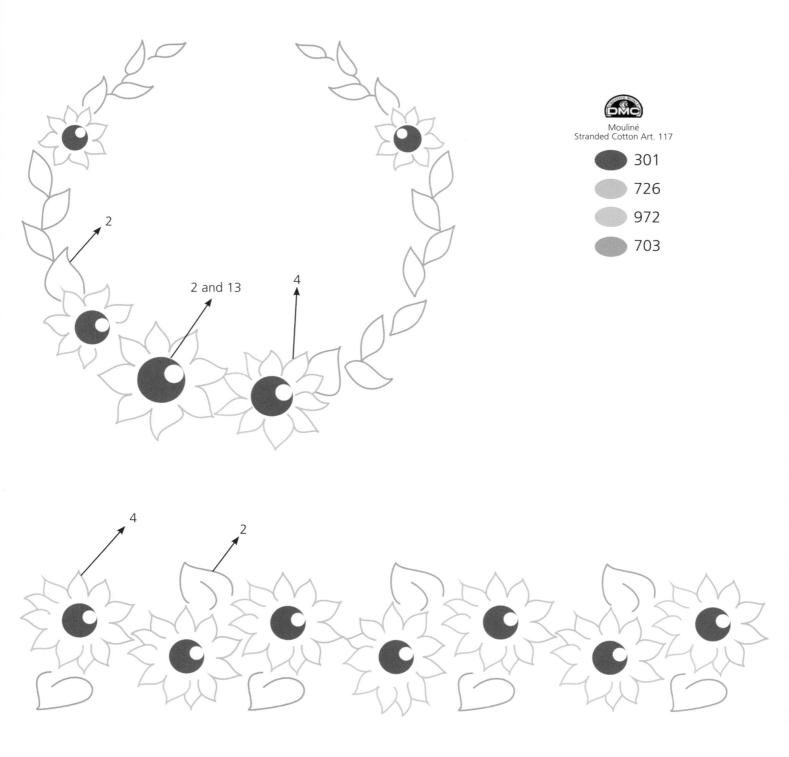

Mouliné
Stranded Cotton Art. 117

301
726
972
703

2

2 and 13

4

4

2

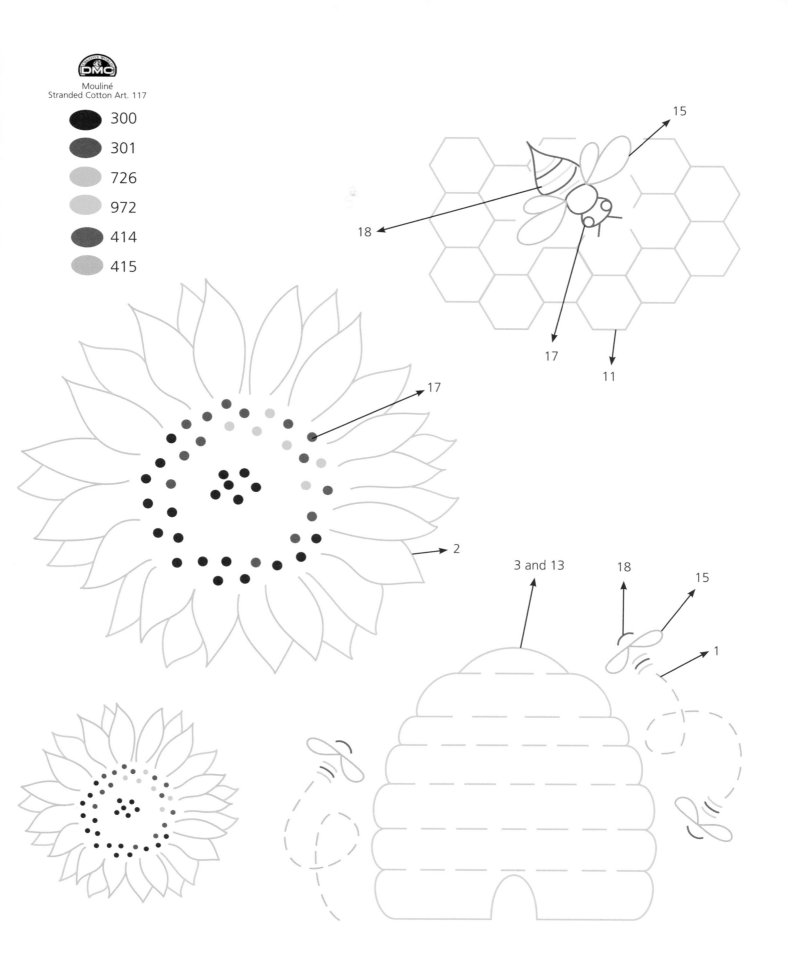

Mouliné
Stranded Cotton Art. 117

300
301
726
972
414
415

15

18

17

11

17

2

3 and 13

18

15

1

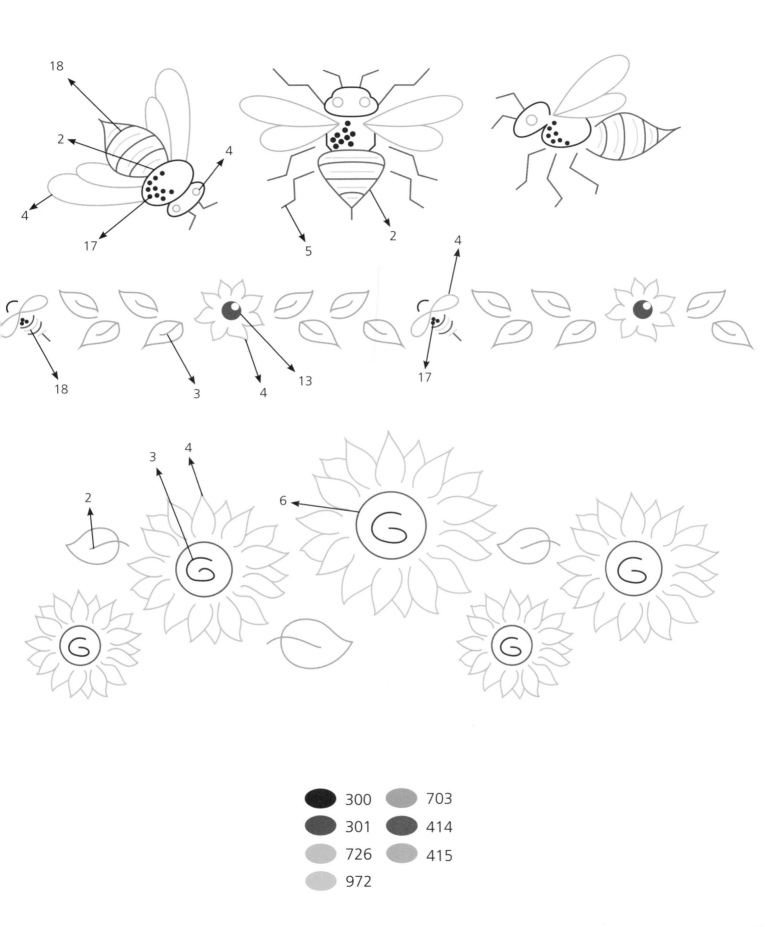

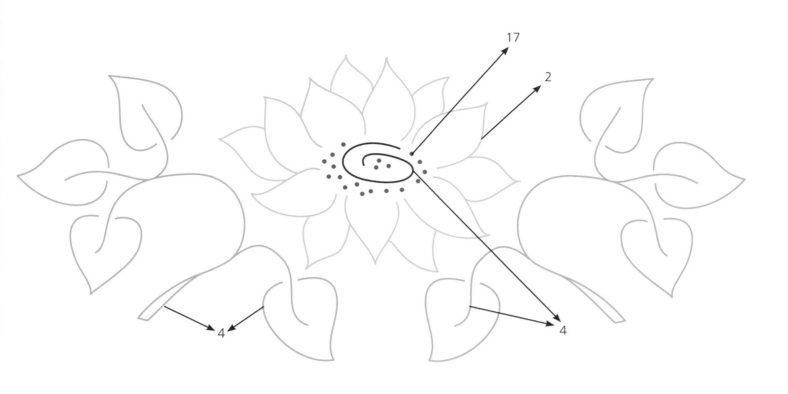

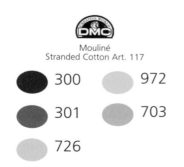

Mouliné
Stranded Cotton Art. 117

- 300
- 972
- 301
- 703
- 726

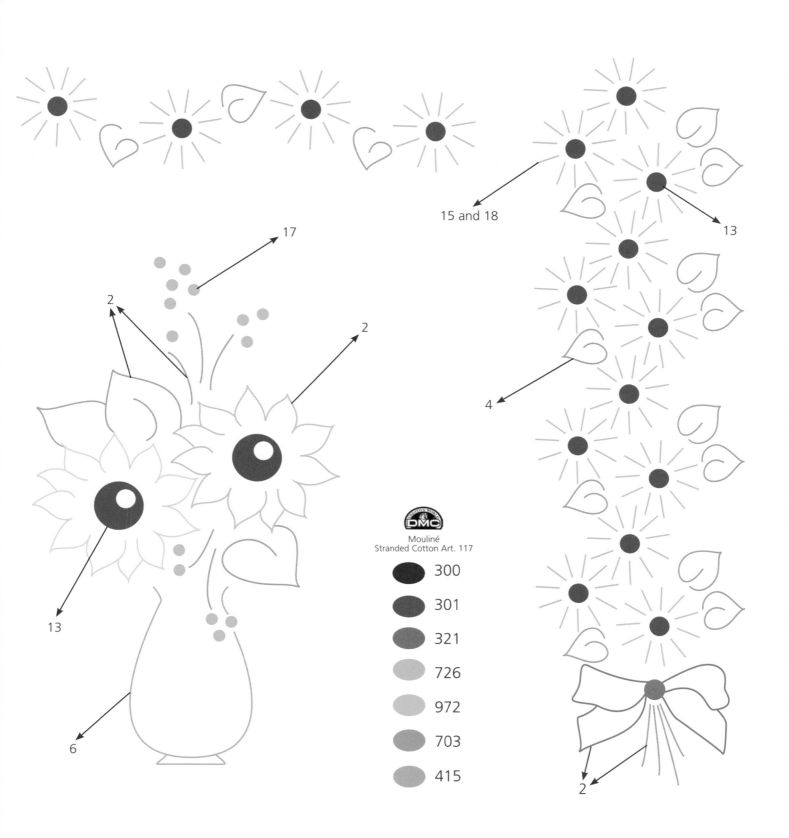

17

2

2

15 and 18

13

4

13

6

DMC
Mouliné
Stranded Cotton Art. 117

300
301
321
726
972
703
415

2

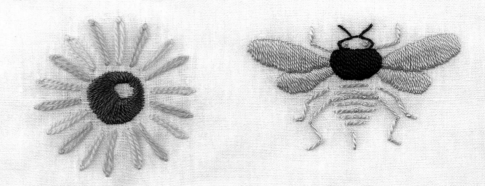

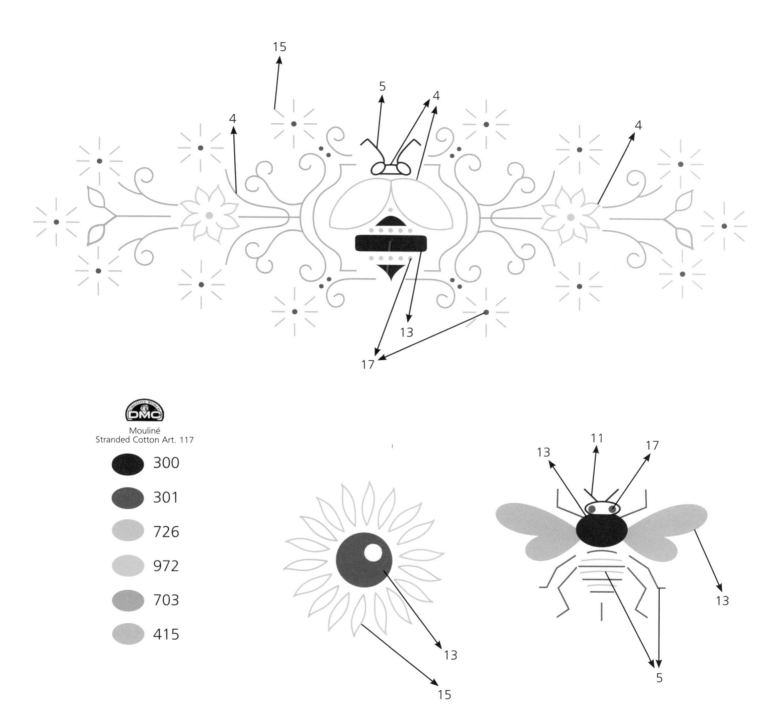

Mouliné
Stranded Cotton Art. 117

300

301

726

972

703

415

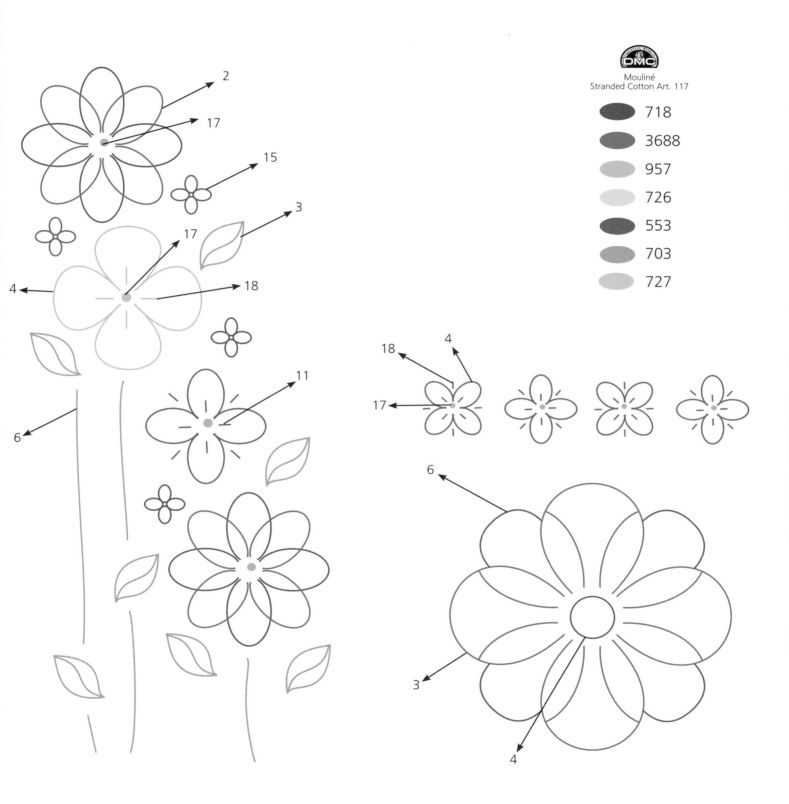

Mouliné
Stranded Cotton Art. 117

718 726
3688 553
957 703

Mouliné
Stranded Cotton Art. 117

209
602
333
726
340
703
702

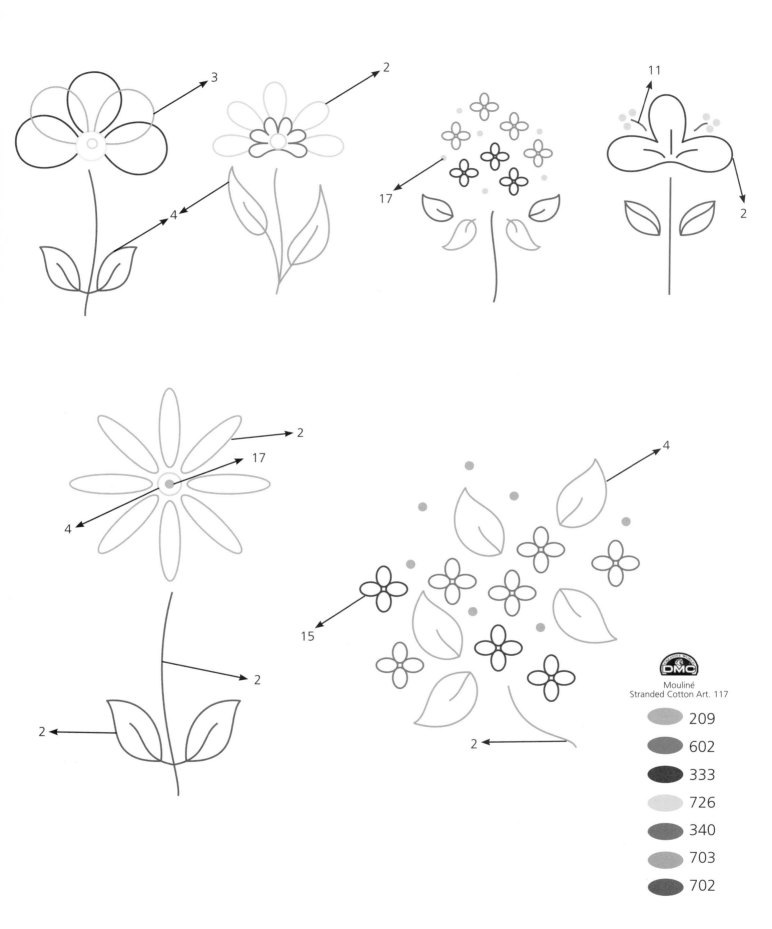

Mouliné
Stranded Cotton Art. 117

209
602
333
726
340
703
702

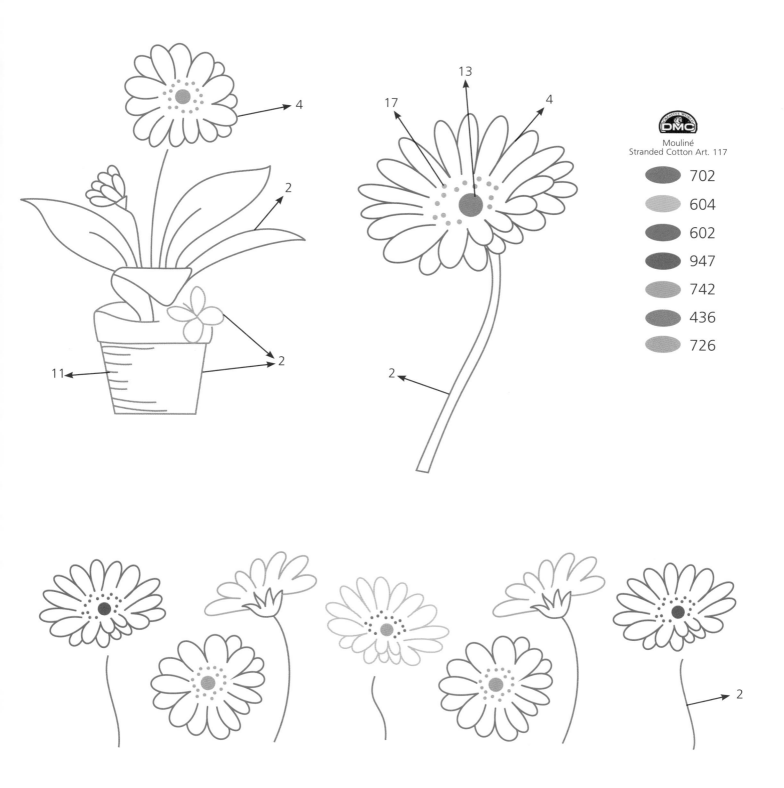

Mouliné
Stranded Cotton Art. 117

702
604
602
947
742
436
726

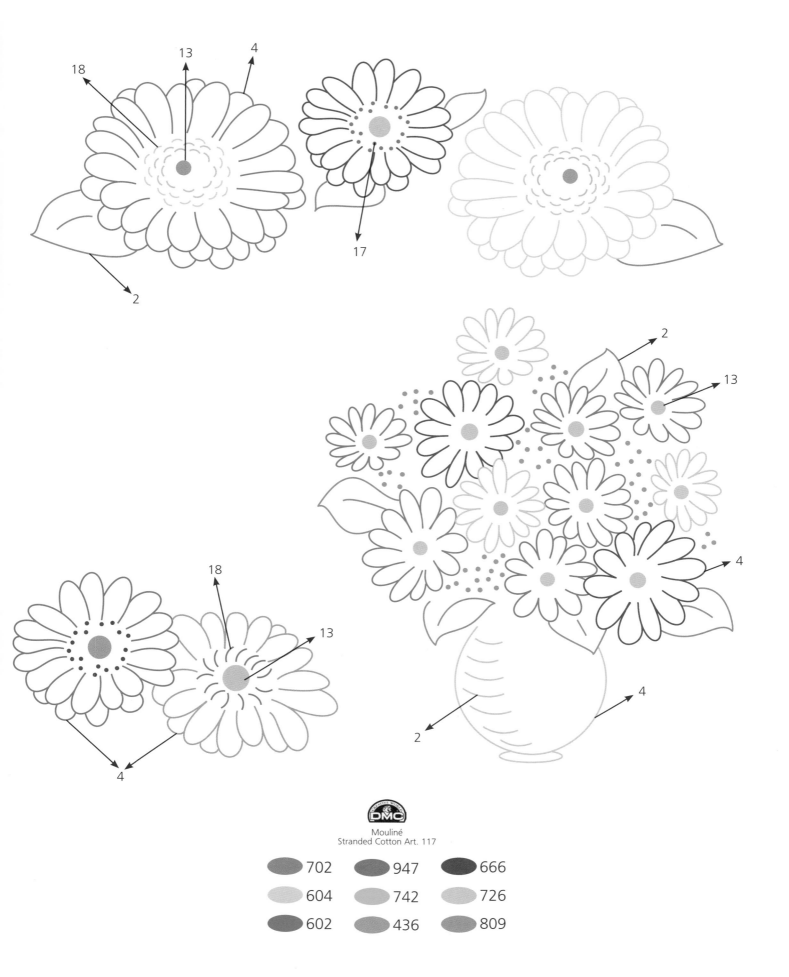

Mouliné
Stranded Cotton Art. 117

702 947 666
604 742 726
602 436 809

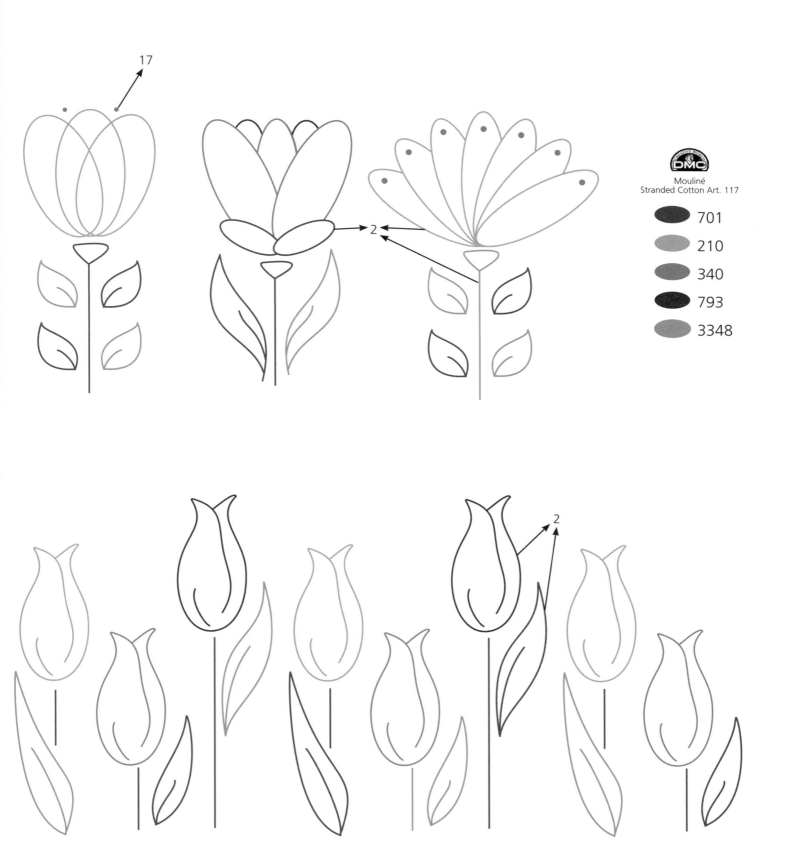

17

2

Mouliné
Stranded Cotton Art. 117

701
210
340
793
3348

2

Mouliné
Stranded Cotton Art. 117

701
210
333

51

Mouliné
Stranded Cotton Art. 117

703
809
797
3348

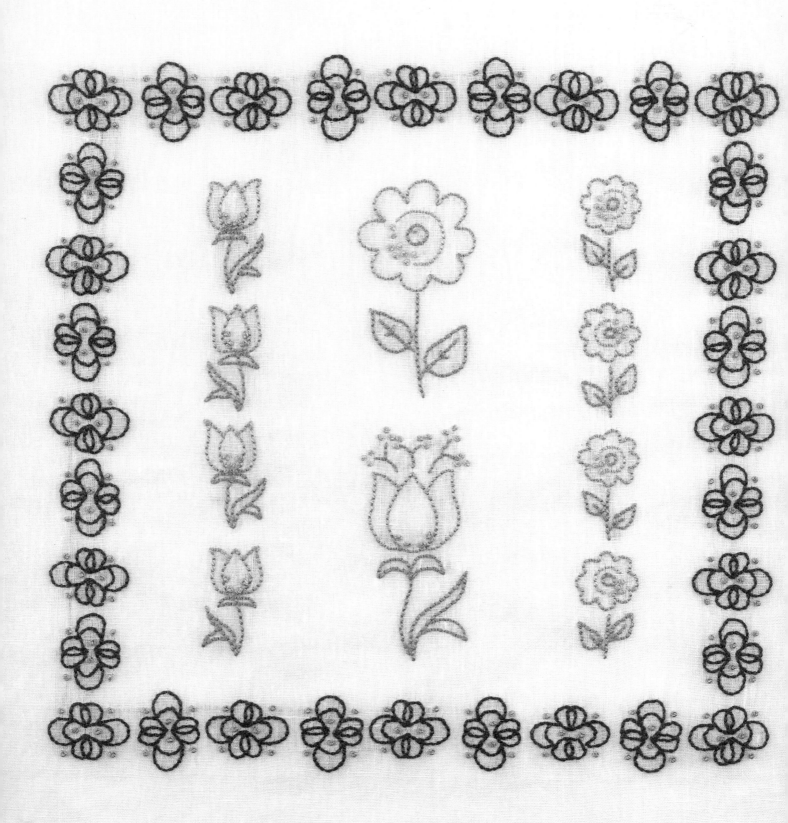

Mouliné
Stranded Cotton Art. 117

703 797
809 3348

17

13

4

13

4

4

4

Mouliné
Stranded Cotton Art. 117

943

744

742

3348

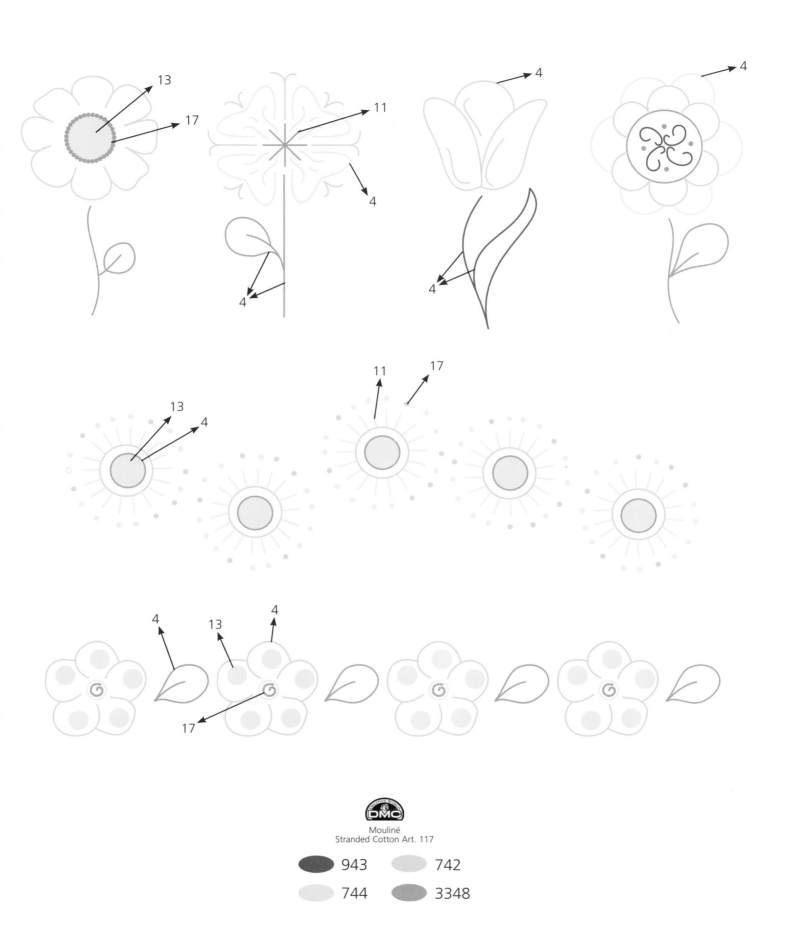

Mouliné
Stranded Cotton Art. 117

943   742
744   3348

Mouliné
Stranded Cotton Art. 117

744   666
742   340
740   793
3346

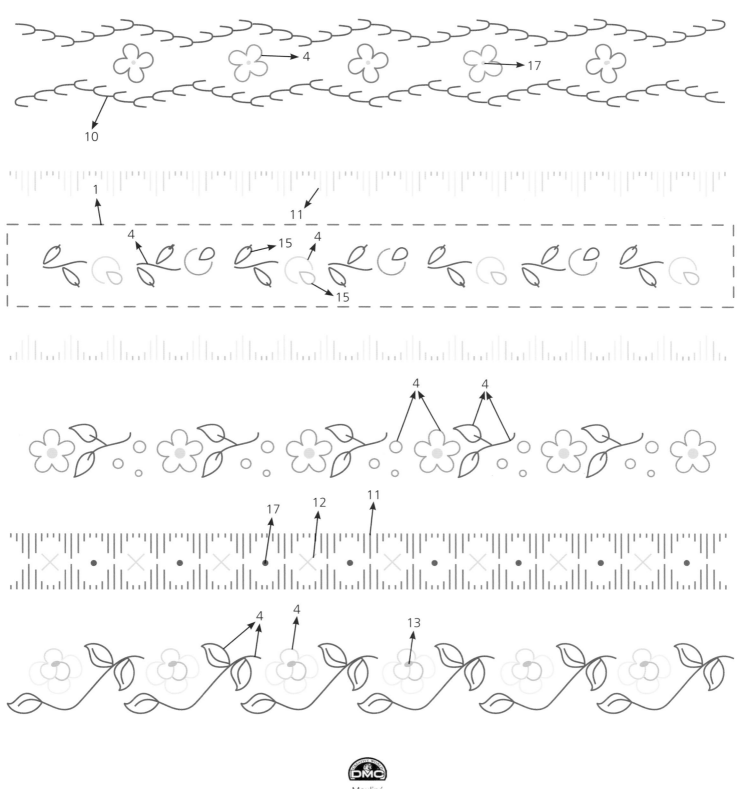

Mouliné
Stranded Cotton Art. 117

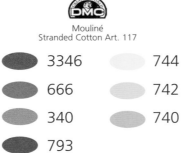

3346   744

666   742

340   740

793

Mouliné
Stranded Cotton Art. 117

⬭	744	⬬	3346	⬬	793
⬬	742	⬬	666		
⬬	740	⬬	340		

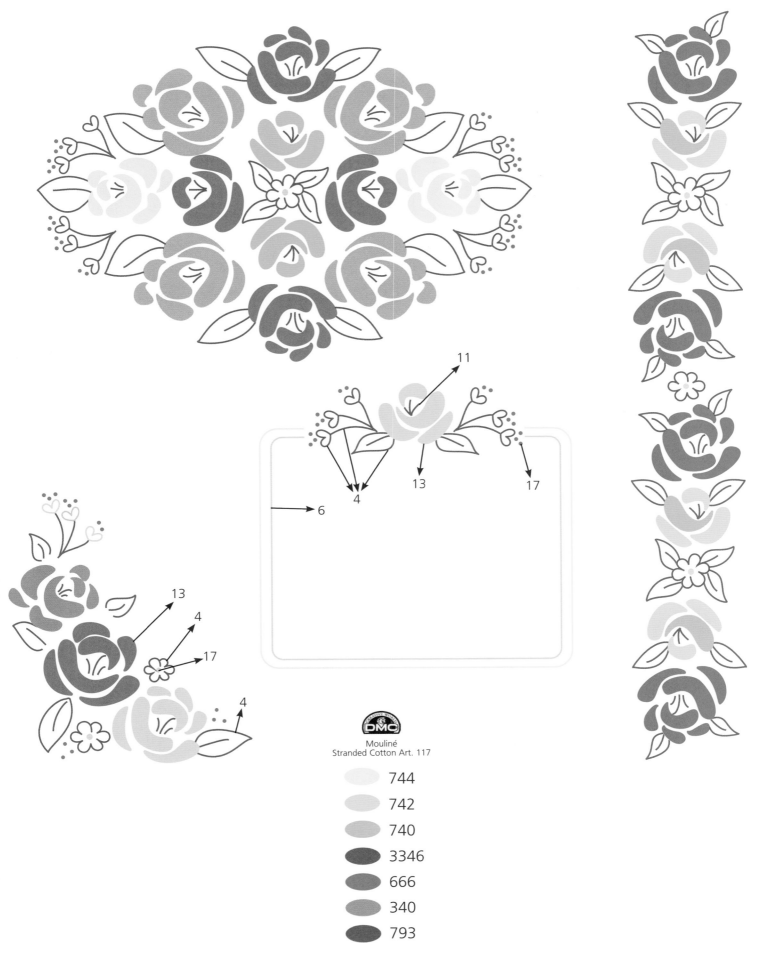

Mouliné
Stranded Cotton Art. 117

744
742
740
3346
666
340
793

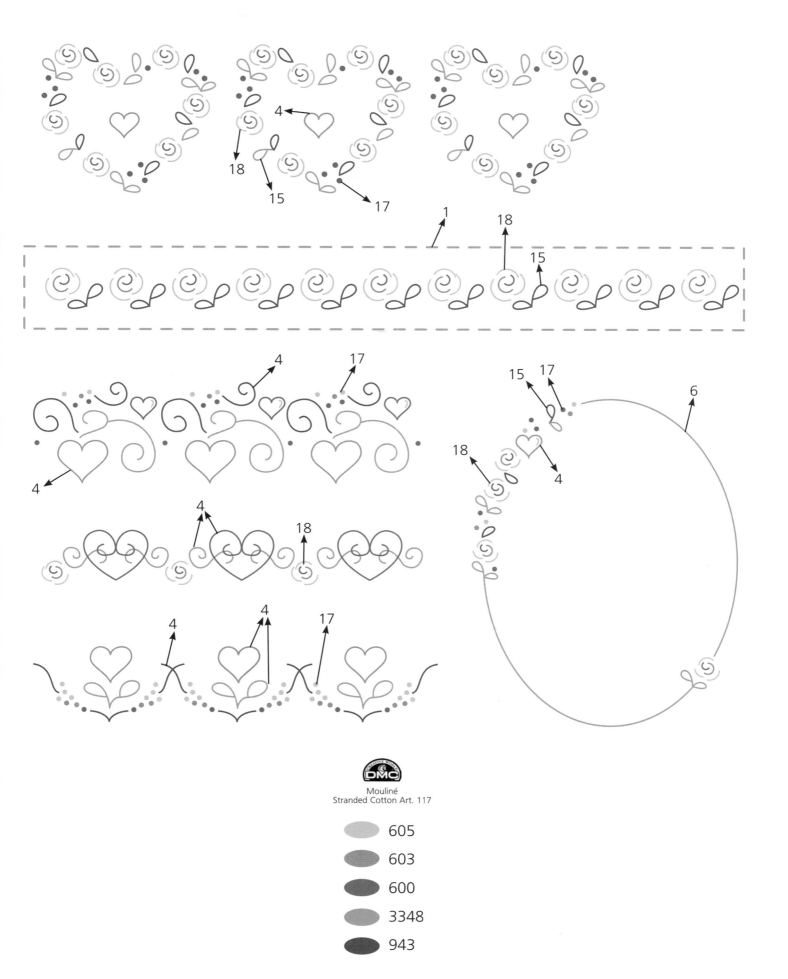

Mouliné
Stranded Cotton Art. 117

605
603
600
3348
943

Mouliné
Stranded Cotton Art. 117

605		3348	
603		943	
600			

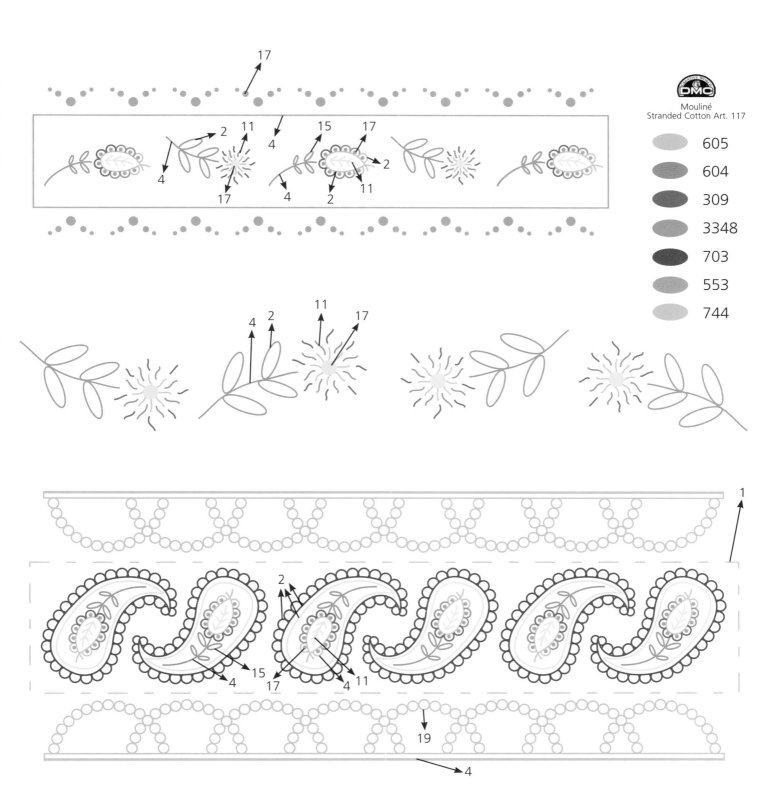

Mouliné
Stranded Cotton Art. 117

605
604
309
3348
703
553
744

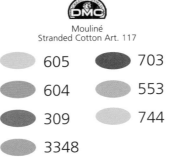

Mouliné
Stranded Cotton Art. 117

605		703	
604		553	
309		744	
3348			

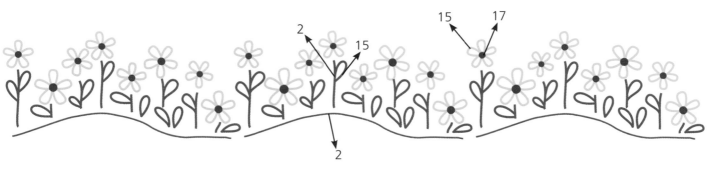

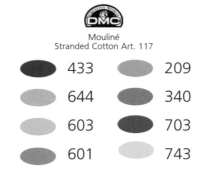

Mouliné
Stranded Cotton Art. 117

433		209	
644		340	
603		703	
601		743	

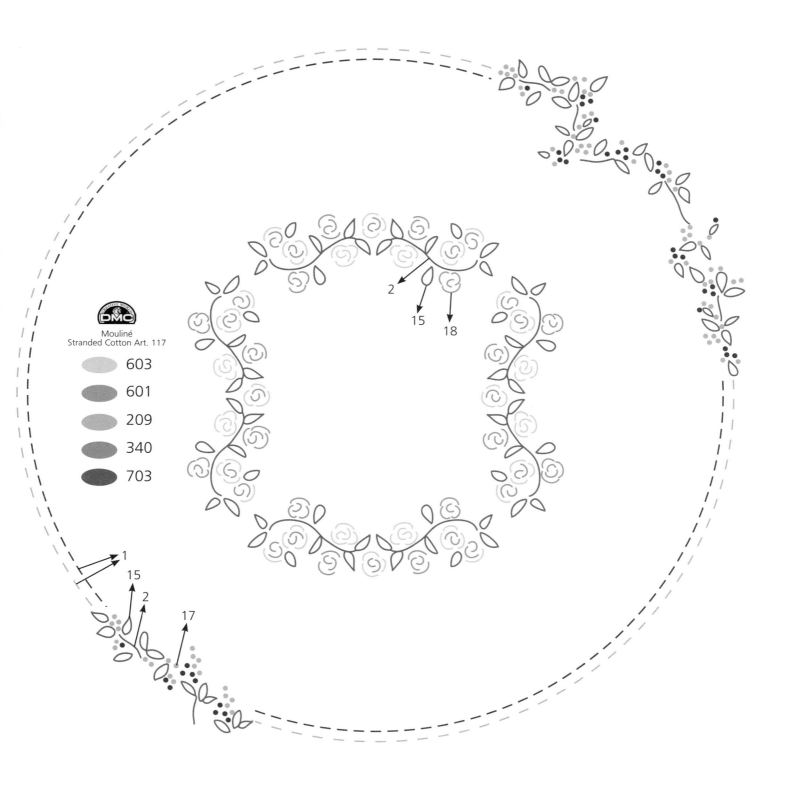

Mouliné
Stranded Cotton Art. 117

603
601
209
340
703

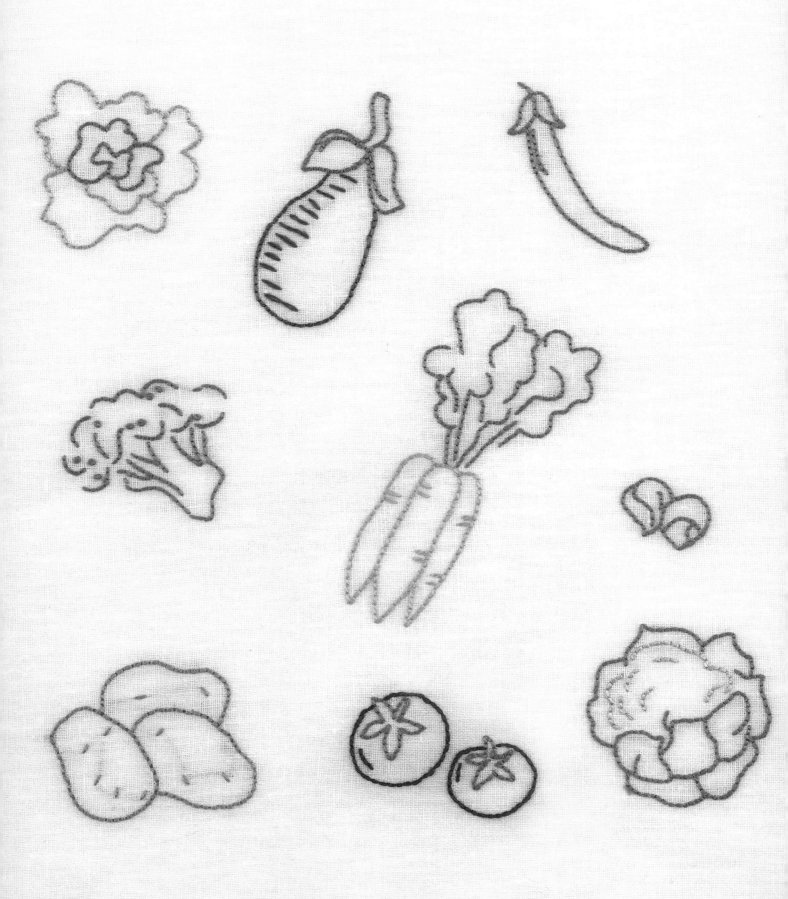

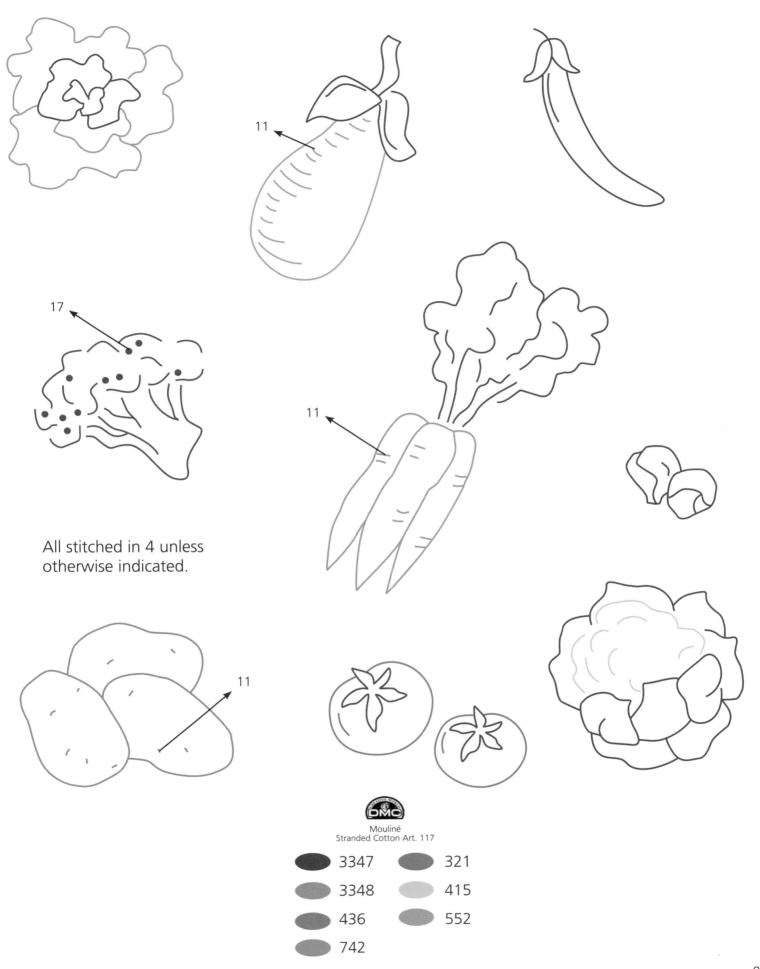

All stitched in 4 unless
otherwise indicated.

Mouliné
Stranded Cotton Art. 117

3347   321
3348   415
436   552
742

81

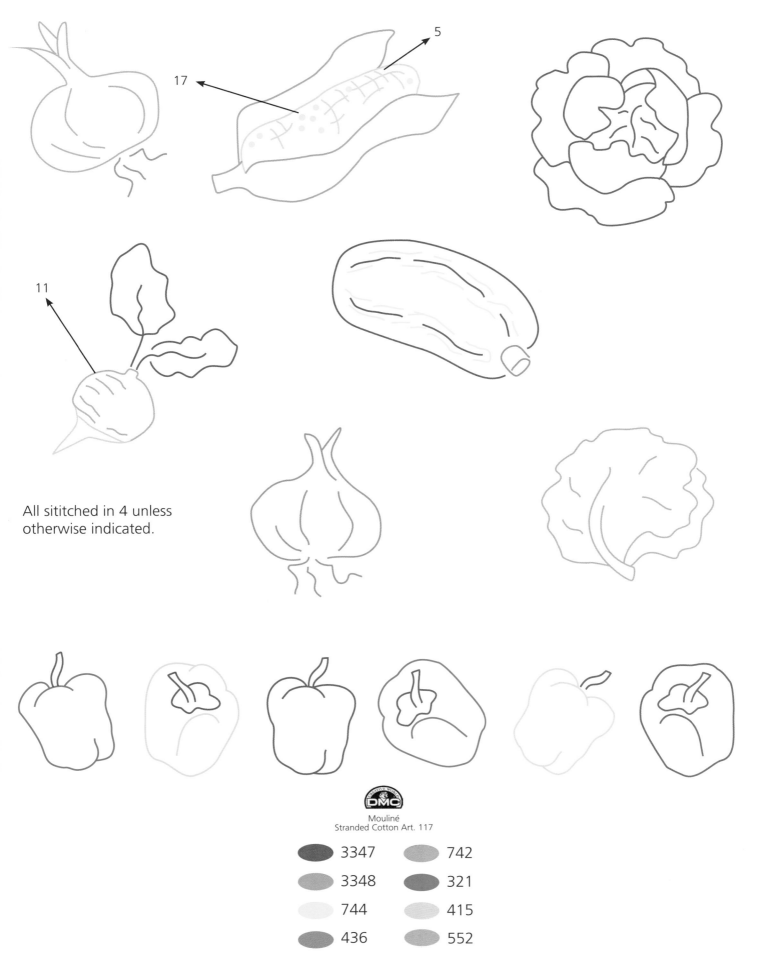

5

17

11

All sititched in 4 unless
otherwise indicated.

Mouliné
Stranded Cotton Art. 117

●	3347	●	742
●	3348	●	321
●	744	●	415
●	436	●	552

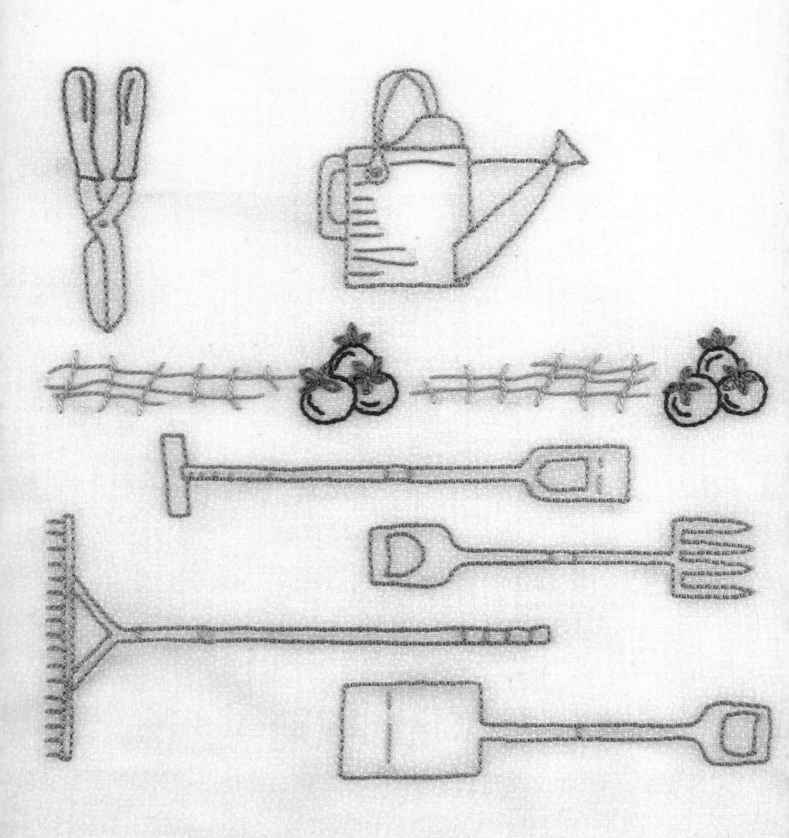

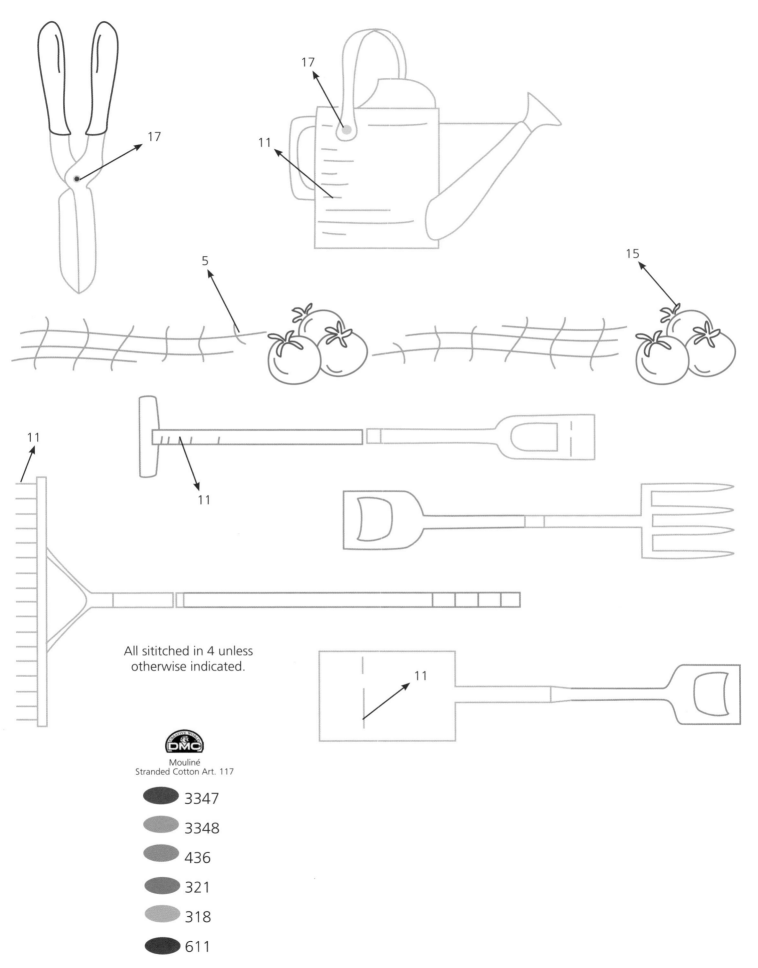

17

17

11

5

15

11

11

All sititched in 4 unless
otherwise indicated.

11

DMC
Mouliné
Stranded Cotton Art. 117

3347

3348

436

321

318

611

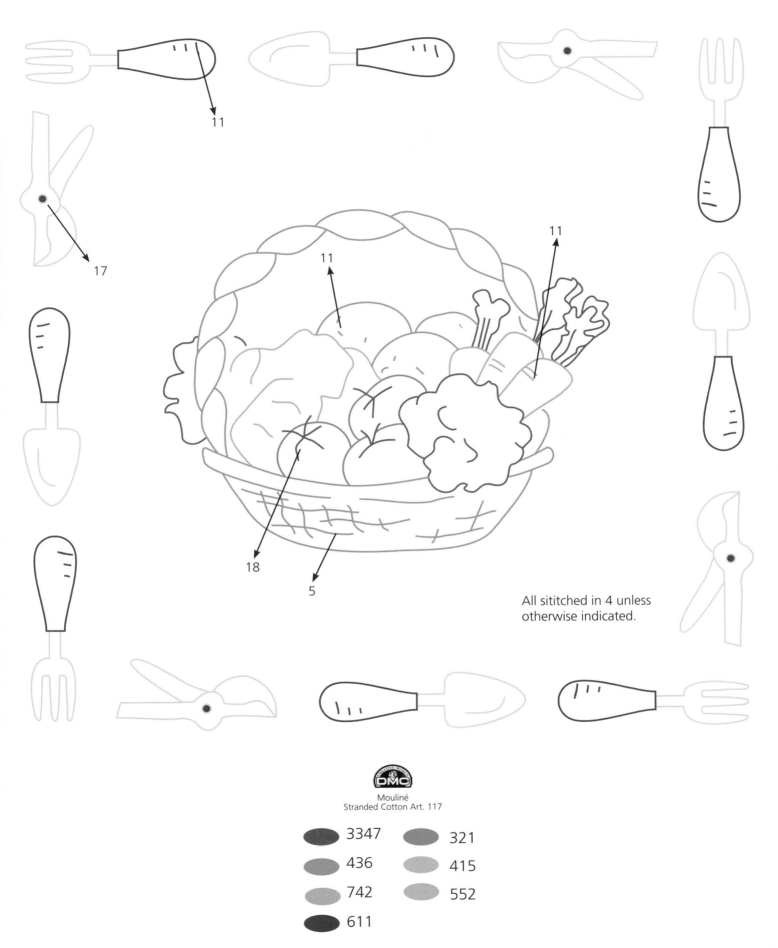

All sititched in 4 unless
otherwise indicated.

Mouliné
Stranded Cotton Art. 117

3347   321
436   415
742   552
611

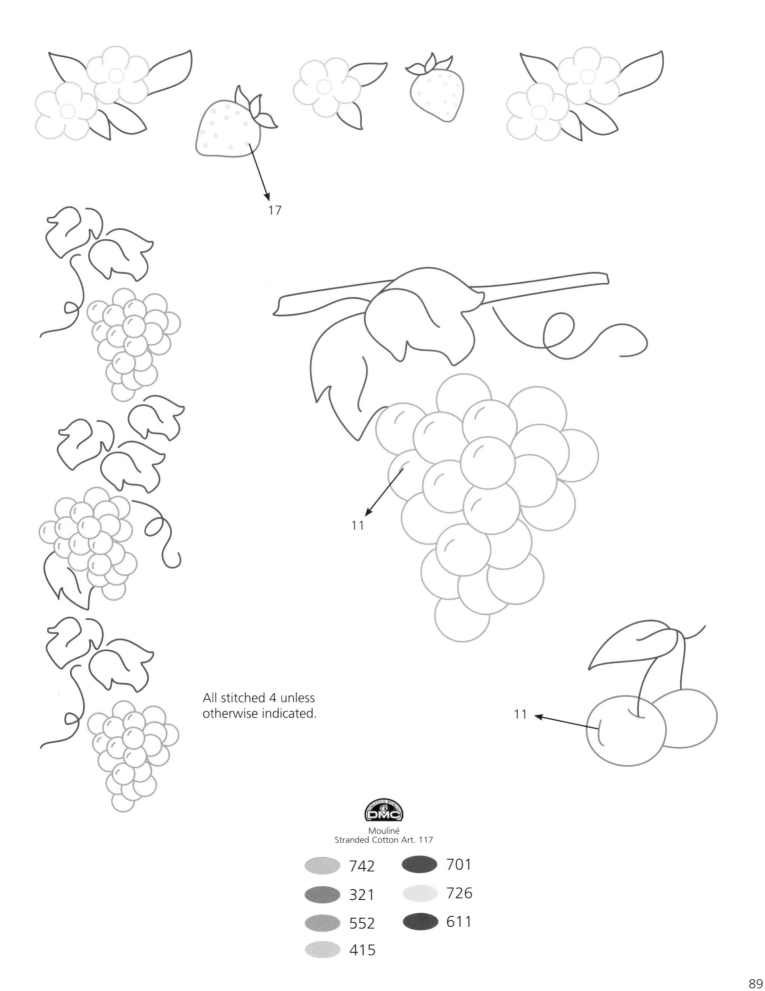

17

11

All stitched 4 unless
otherwise indicated.

11

Mouliné
Stranded Cotton Art. 117

742   701

321   726

552   611

415

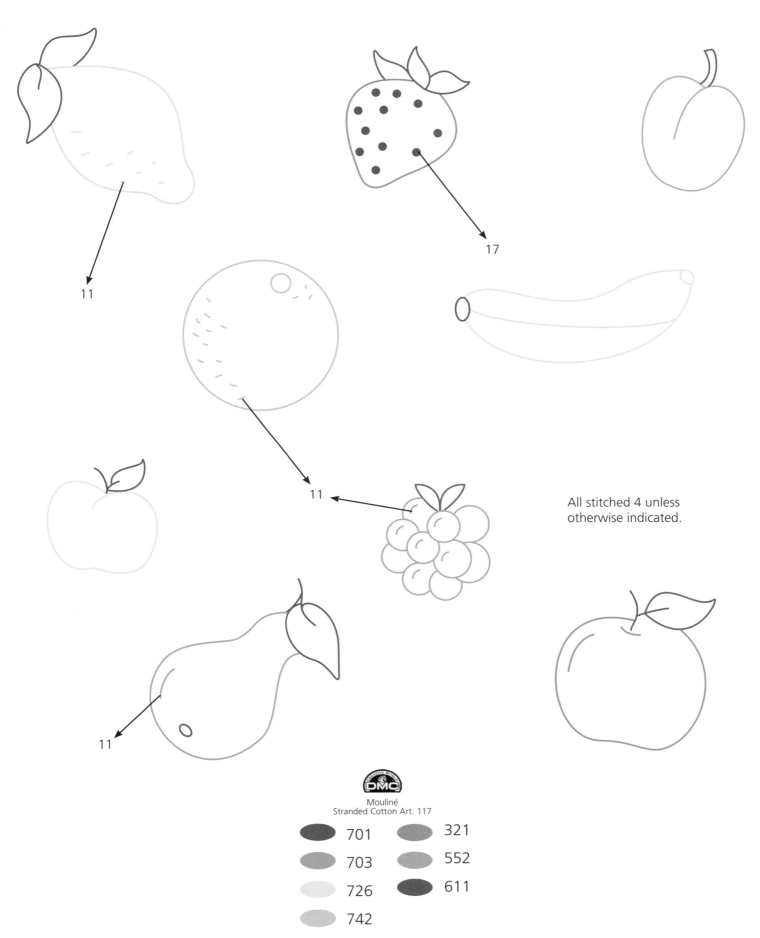

11

17

11

All stitched 4 unless
otherwise indicated.

11

DMC

Mouliné
Stranded Cotton Art. 117

701   321

703   552

726   611

742

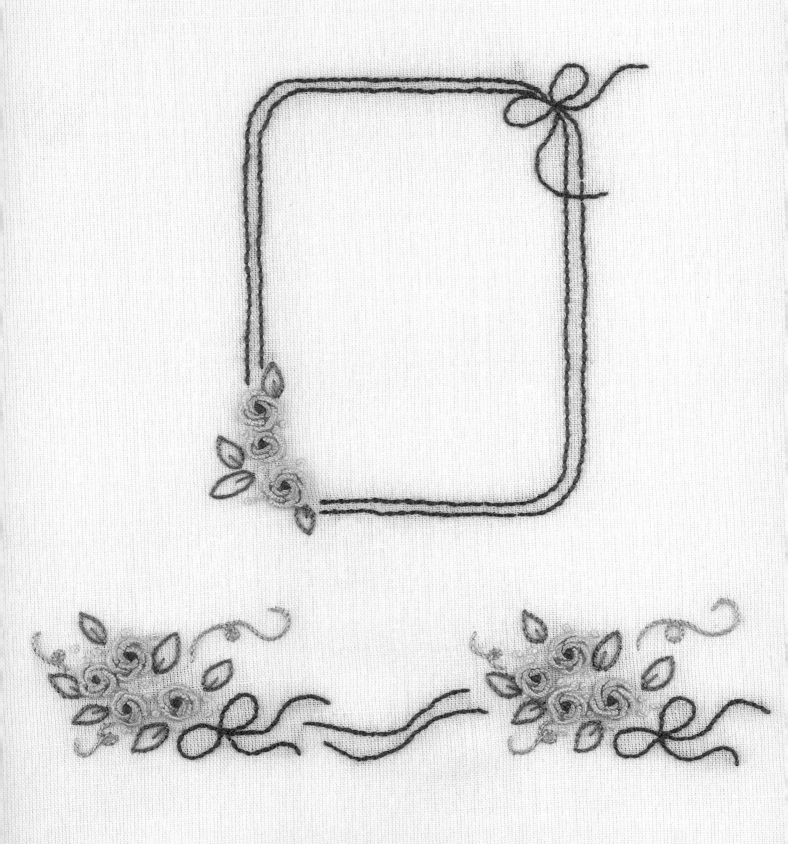

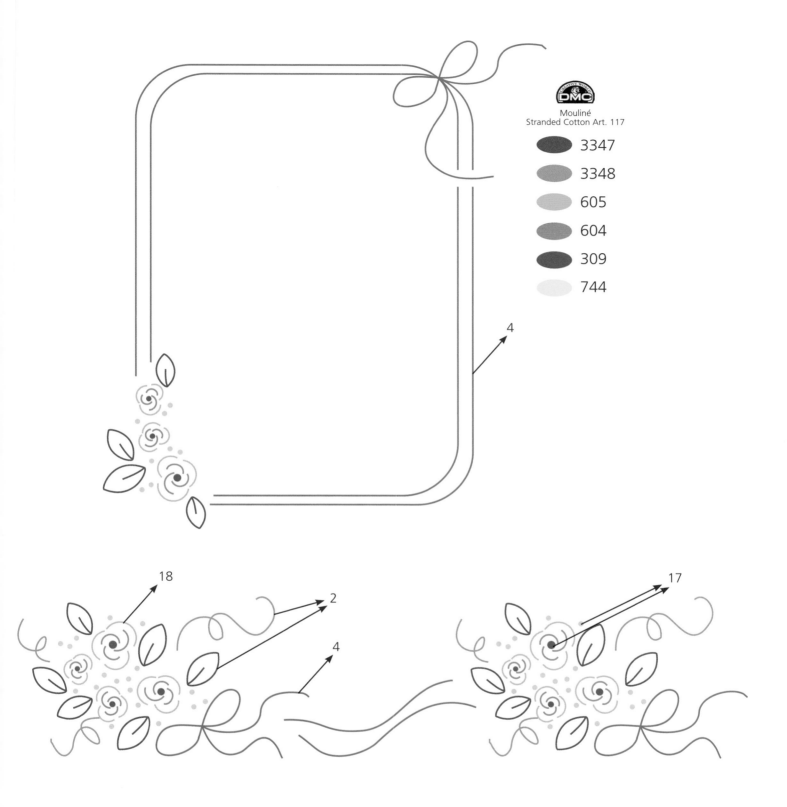

Mouliné
Stranded Cotton Art. 117

3347
3348
605
604
309
744

4

18

2

4

17

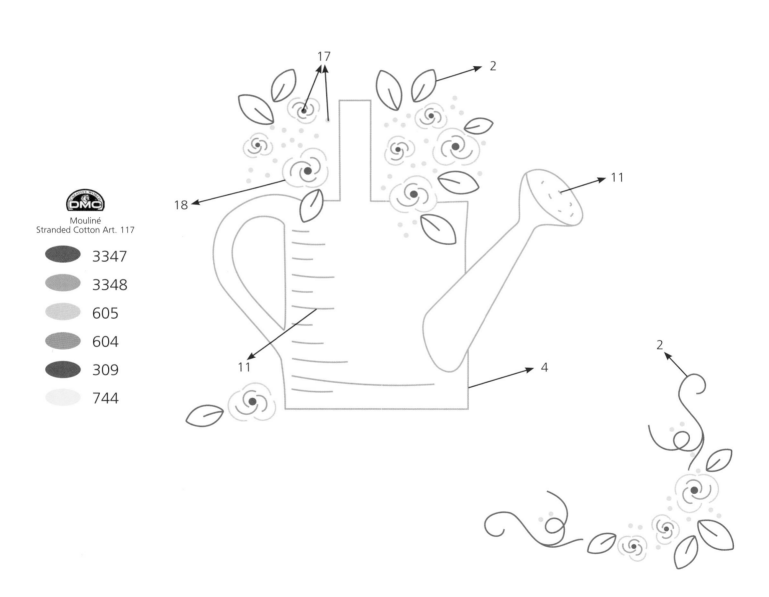

Mouliné
Stranded Cotton Art. 117

3347
3348
605
604
309
744

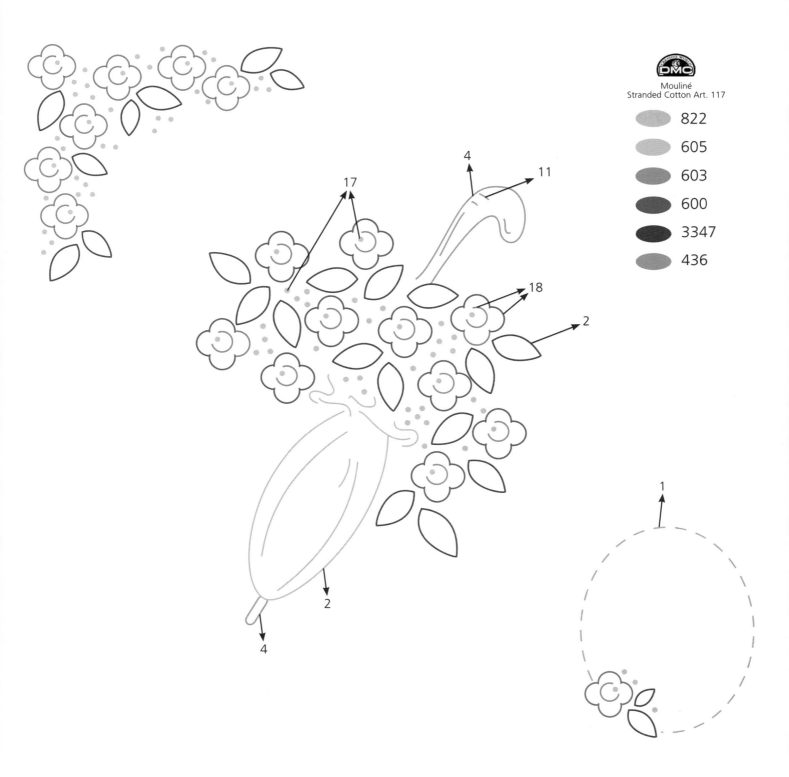

Mouliné
Stranded Cotton Art. 117

822
605
603
600
3347
436

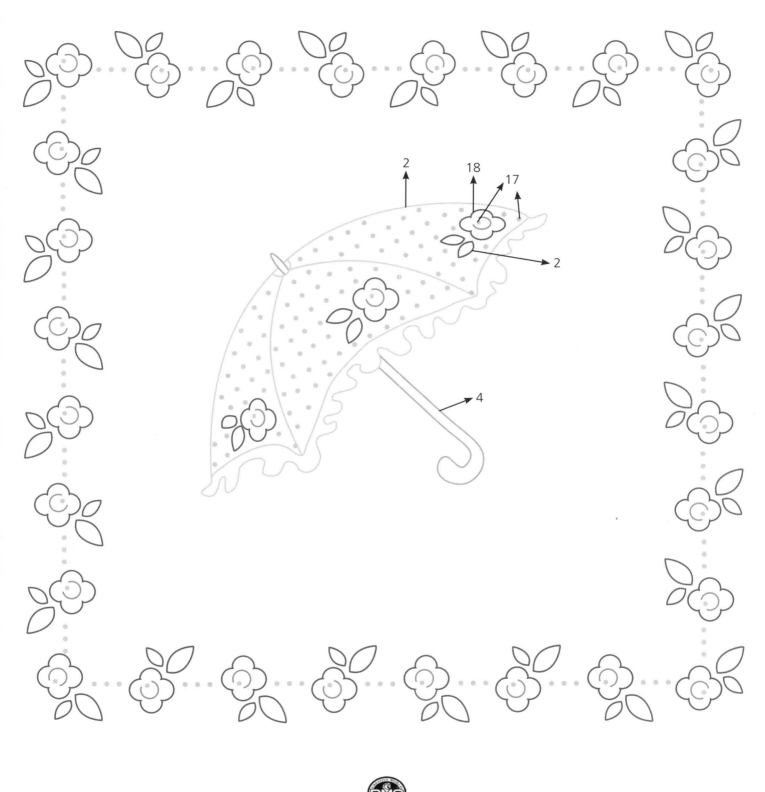

2

18

17

2

4

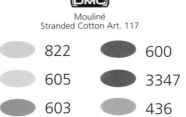

Mouliné
Stranded Cotton Art. 117

⬭	822	⬭	600
⬭	605	⬭	3347
⬭	603	⬭	436

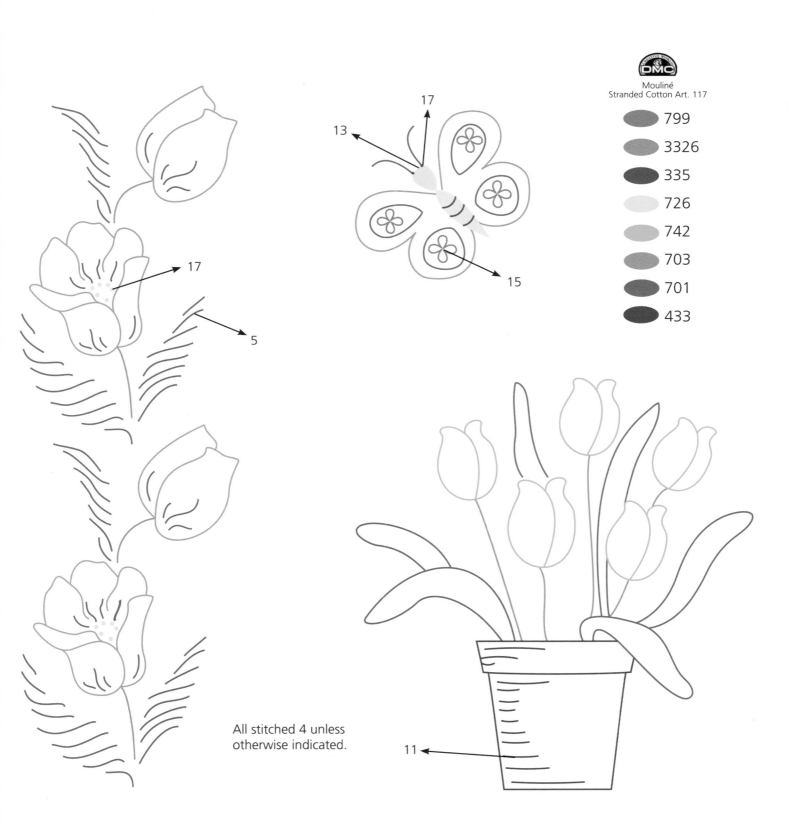

Mouliné
Stranded Cotton Art. 117

799
3326
335
726
742
703
701
433

17

13

15

17

5

All stitched 4 unless
otherwise indicated.

11

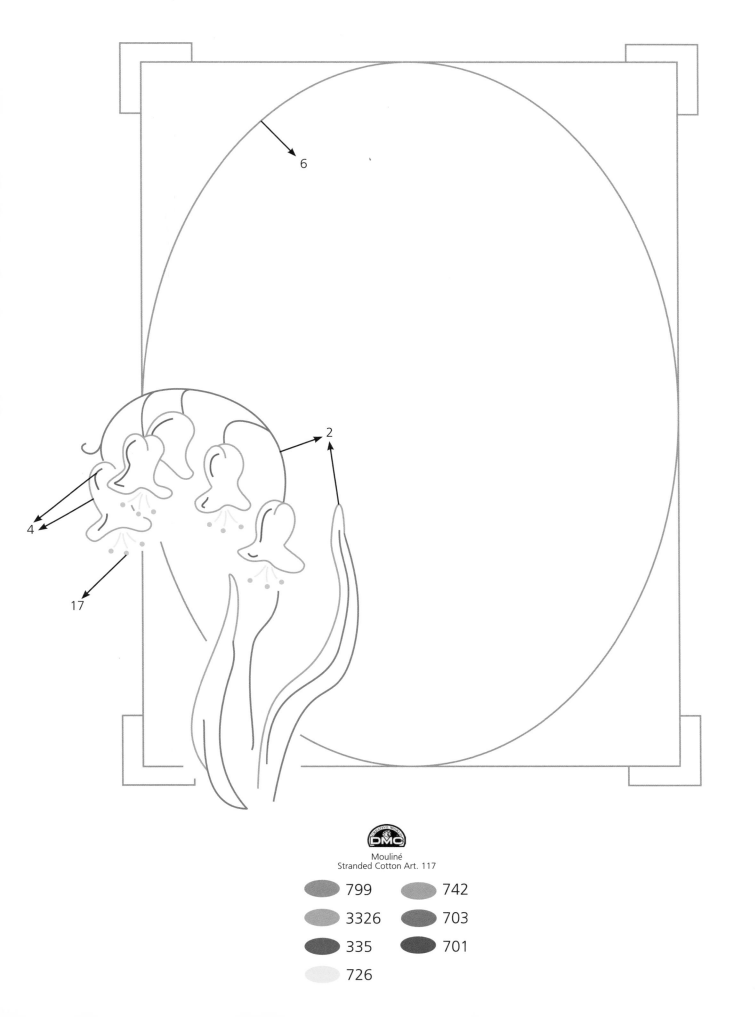

Mouliné
Stranded Cotton Art. 117

799 742
3326 703
335 701
726

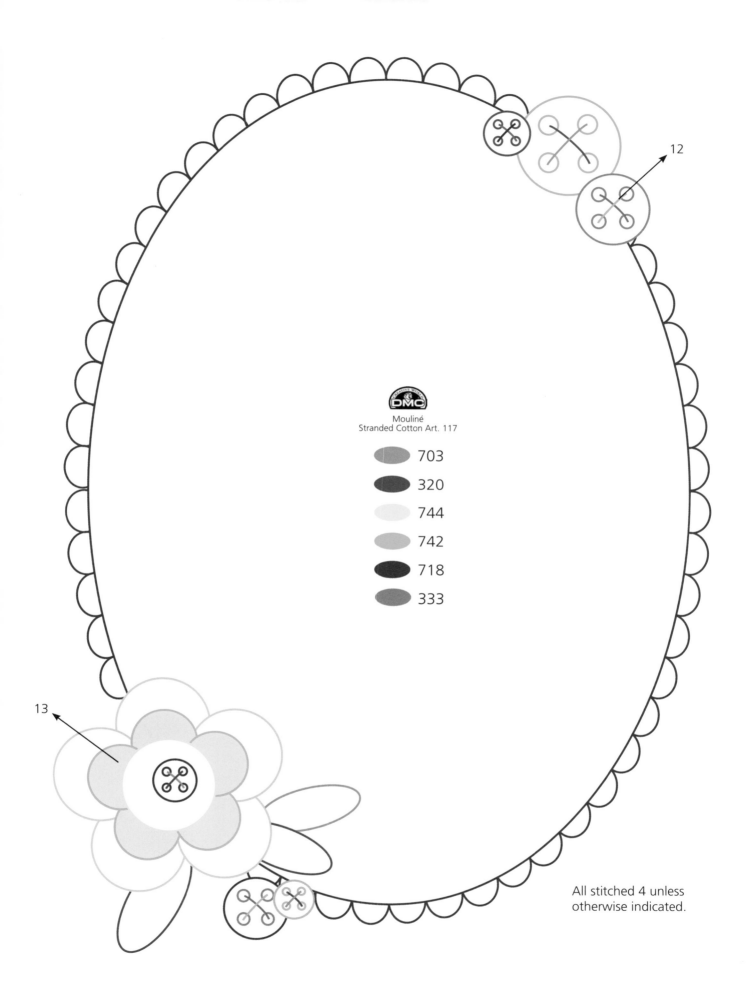

DMC
Mouliné
Stranded Cotton Art. 117

703
320
744
742
718
333

12

13

All stitched 4 unless
otherwise indicated.

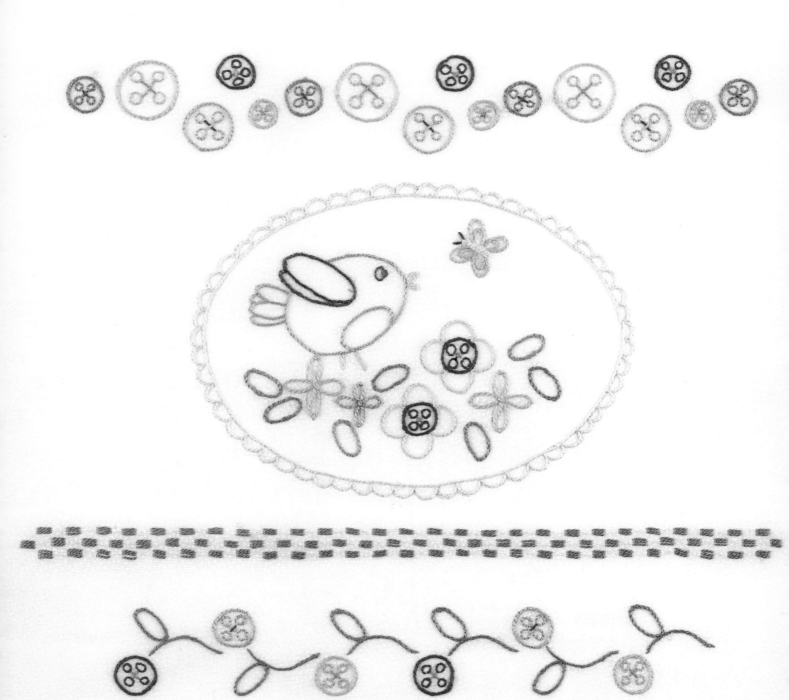

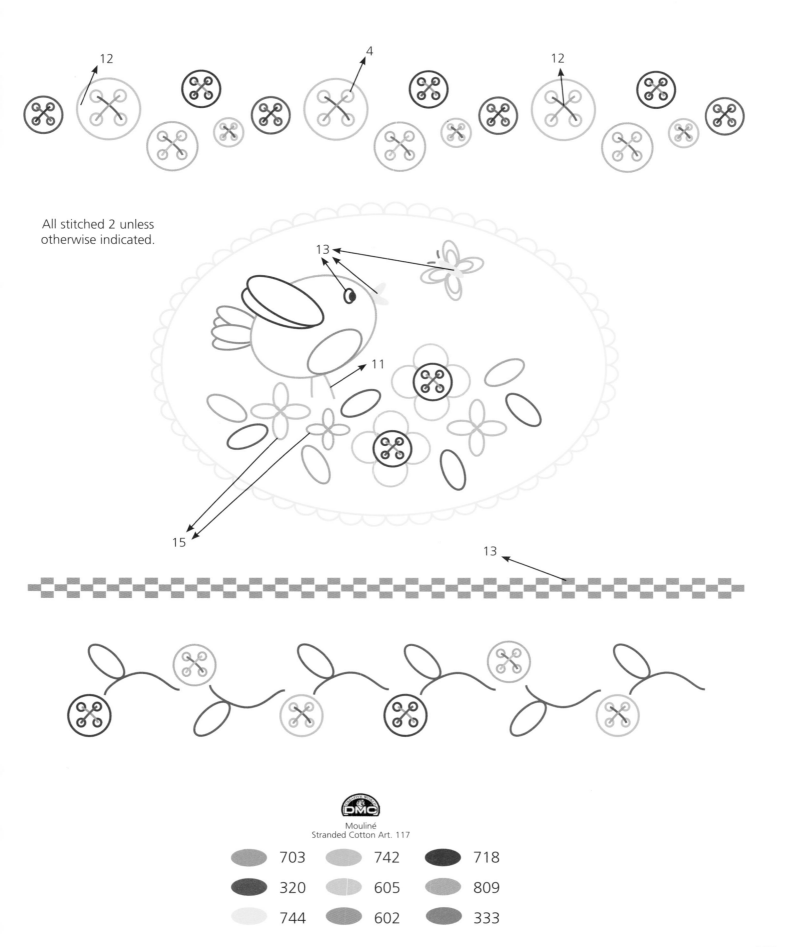

All stitched 2 unless
otherwise indicated.

DMC
Mouliné
Stranded Cotton Art. 117

703   742   718
320   605   809
744   602   333

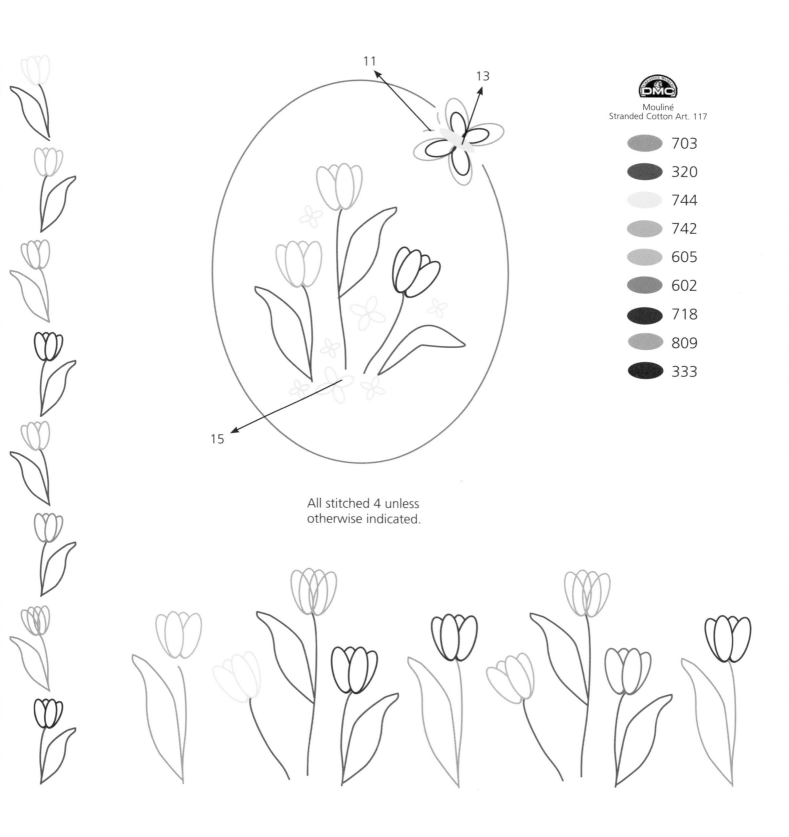

All stitched 4 unless
otherwise indicated.

Mouliné
Stranded Cotton Art. 117

703
320
744
742
605
602
718
809
333

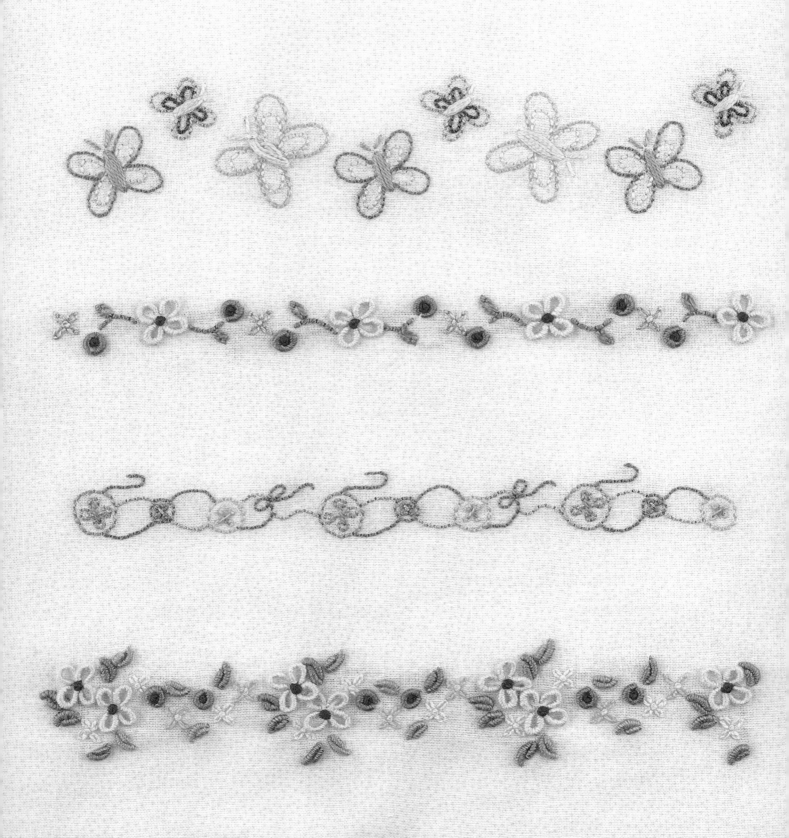

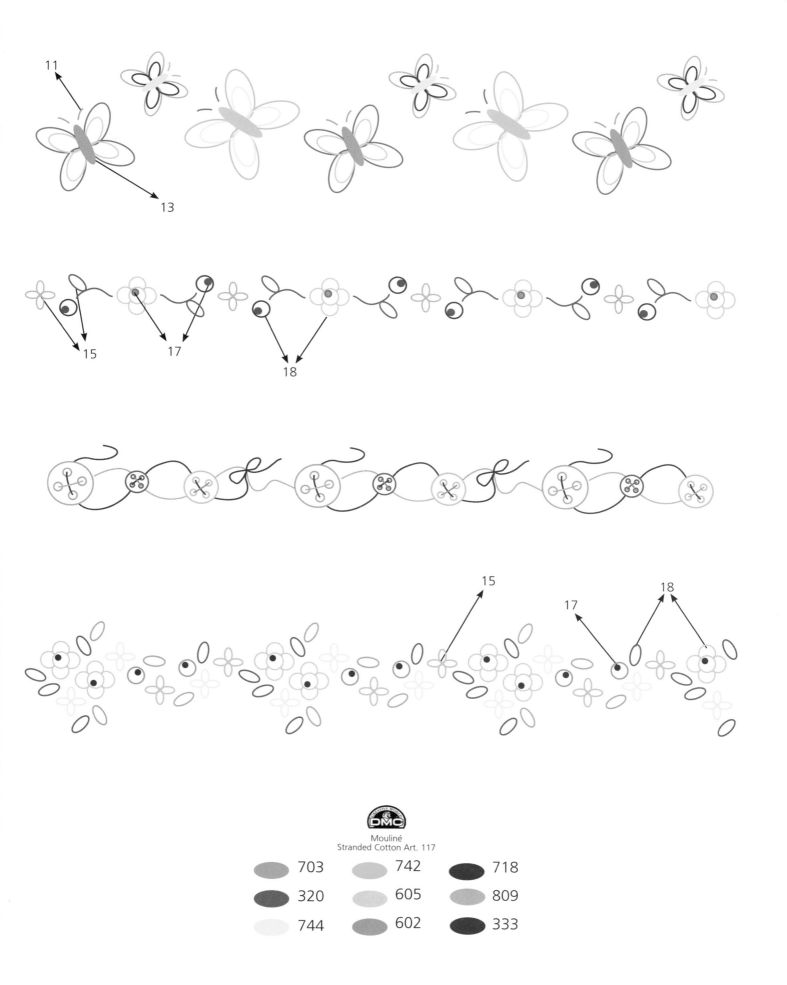

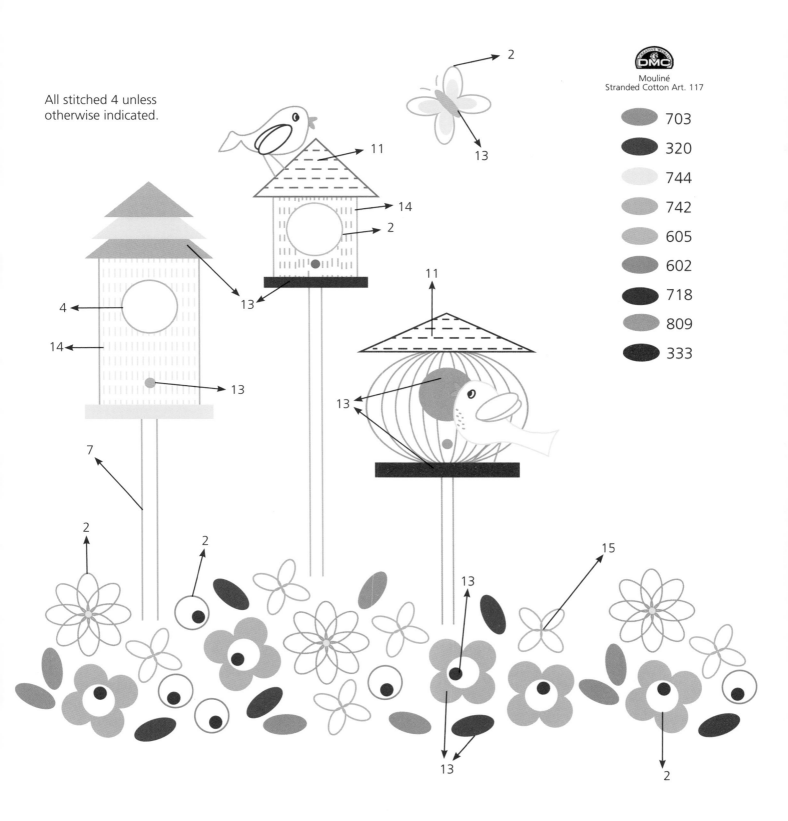

All stitched 4 unless
otherwise indicated.

Mouliné
Stranded Cotton Art. 117

703
320
744
742
605
602
718
809
333

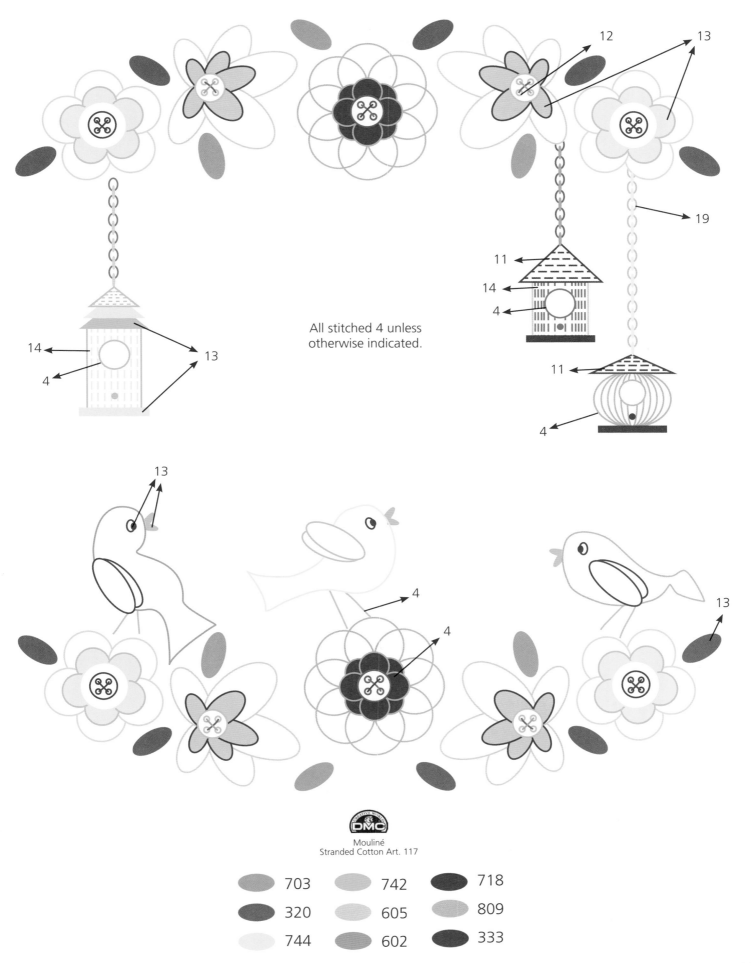

All stitched 4 unless otherwise indicated.

DMC

Mouliné
Stranded Cotton Art. 117

	703		742		718
	320		605		809
	744		602		333

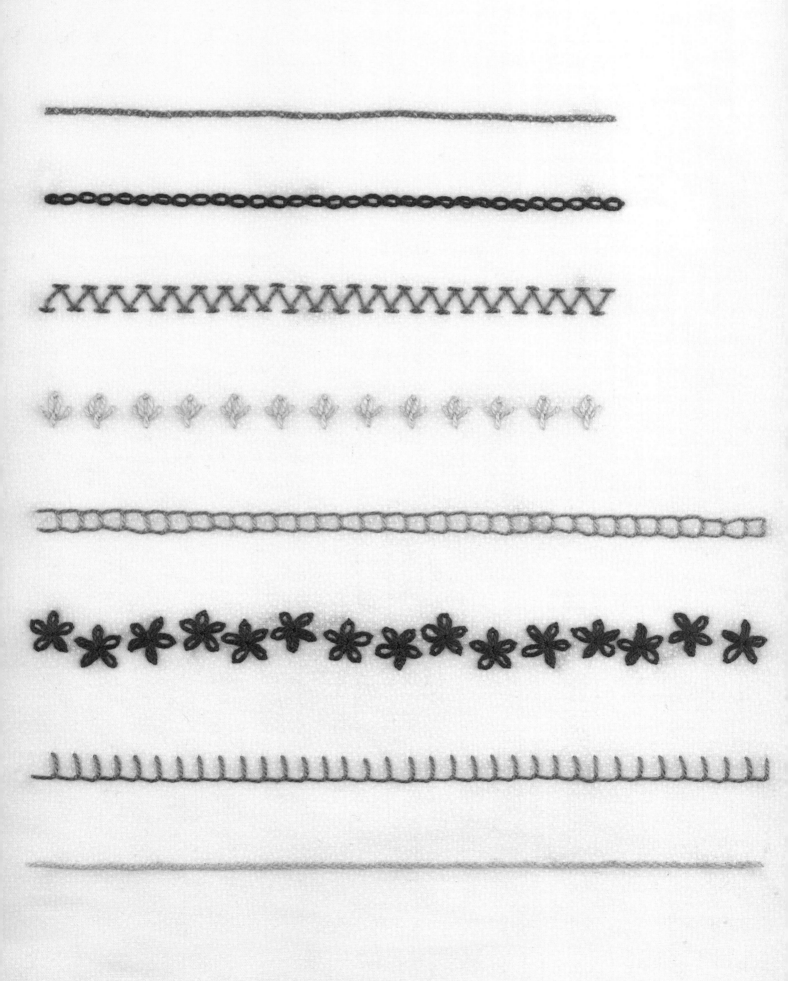

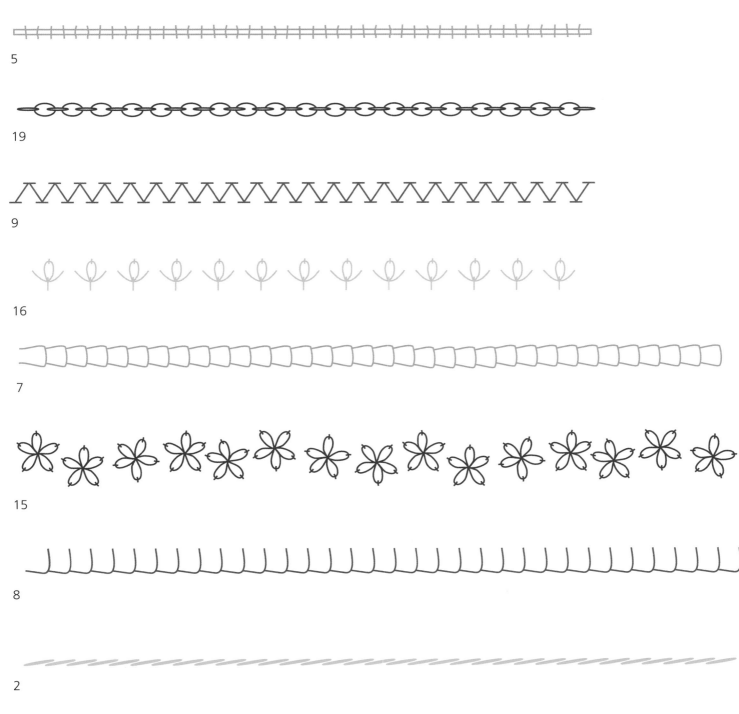

5

19

9

16

7

15

8

2

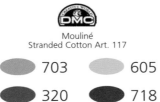

Mouliné
Stranded Cotton Art. 117

703   605

320   718

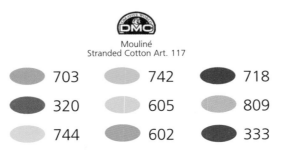

Mouliné
Stranded Cotton Art. 117

	703		742		718
	320		605		809
	744		602		333

All stitched 4 unless otherwise indicated.

Mouliné
Stranded Cotton Art. 117

703
320
744
742
605
602
436
433
3325

All stitched 4 unless
otherwise indicated.

Mouliné
Stranded Cotton Art. 117

703
320
744
742
605
602
436
433
3325
550
209

123

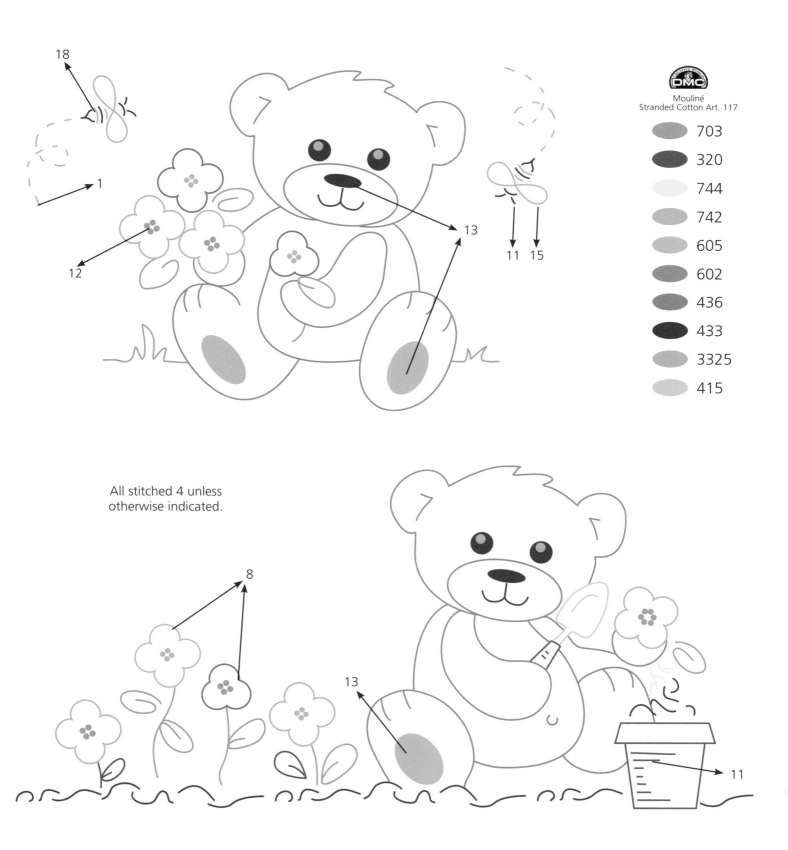

18

1

12

13

11 15

Mouliné
Stranded Cotton Art. 117

703
320
744
742
605
602
436
433
3325
415

All stitched 4 unless
otherwise indicated.

8

13

11

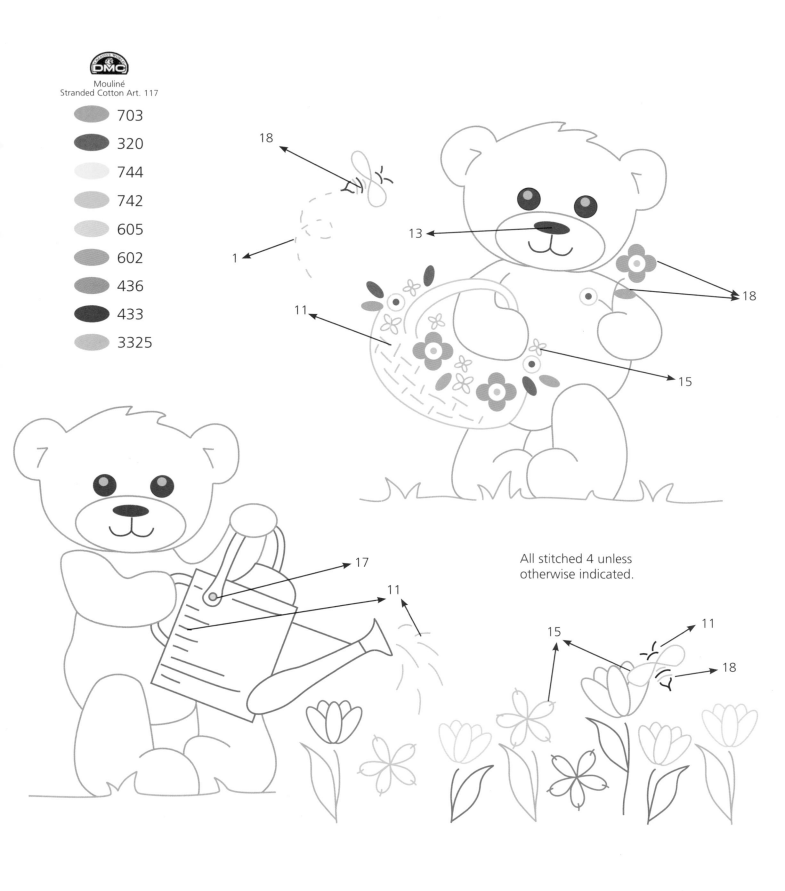

Mouliné
Stranded Cotton Art. 117

703
320
744
742
605
602
436
433
3325

18

1

13

18

11

15

17

11

All stitched 4 unless
otherwise indicated.

15

11

18